JACK PERRY

Zondervan Publishing House
Grand Rapids, Michigan

LIGHT FROM LIGHT is a Daybreak Book
Published by the Zondervan Publishing House
1415 Lake Drive, S.E., Grand Rapids, Michigan 49506

Copyright © 1987 by Jack Perry

All rights reserved. No part of this publication may be reproduced, stored in a retrieval system, or transmitted in any form or by any means—electronic, mechanical, photocopy, recording, or any other—except for brief quotations in printed reviews, without the prior permission of the publisher.

Library of Congress Cataloging in Publication Data

Perry, Jack, 1930–
Light from light: meditations from the mountainside / Jack Perry.
p. cm.
ISBN 0-310-23850-1
1. Sermon on the mount—Meditations. I. Title.
BT380.2.P377 1987   87-20147
226'.906—dc19   CIP

All Scripture is from the King James Version.

Edited by David Hazard and Julie Ackerman Link
Designed by Julie Ackerman Link

Printed in the United States of America

87 88 89 90 91 92 / AH / 9 8 7 6 5 4 3 2 1

To my dearly beloved wife, Elizabeth, the heart and the center of my life.

To my dear children of whom I am so fond, James, Leslie, Jennifer, and Laura, the hope of my life.

To my honored and well-loved mother, Nellie Edwards Perry, a constant inspiration for my life.

To my lovely sister, Jane, a great joy in my life.

And to the memory of my revered father, William Berrian Perry, 1906–1971, a bright light for my life.

Contents

	Foreword	9
Week One	And seeing the multitudes . . . (5:1–2)	13
Week Two	Blessed are the poor in spirit . . . (5:3)	16
Week Three	Blessed are they that mourn . . . (5:4)	19
Week Four	Blessed are the meek . . . (5:5)	23
Week Five	Blessed are they which do hunger and thirst after righteousness . . . (5:6)	27
Week Six	Blessed are the merciful . . . (5:7)	31
Week Seven	Blessed are the pure in heart . . . (5:8)	35
Week Eight	Blessed are the peacemakers . . . (5:9)	39
Week Nine	Blessed are they which are persecuted for righteousness' sake . . . (5:10)	43
Week Ten	Blessed are ye when men shall revile you . . . (5:11–12)	46
Week Eleven	Ye are the salt of the earth . . . (5:13–16)	50
Week Twelve	Think not that I am come to destroy the law . . . (5:17–18)	53
Week Thirteen	Whosoever therefore shall break one of these least commandments . . . (5:19–20)	56
Week Fourteen	. . . Thou shalt not kill . . . (5:21–22)	59
Week Fifteen	Therefore if thou bring thy gift to the altar . . . (5:23–24)	62
Week Sixteen	Agree with thine adversary quickly . . . (5:25–26)	65
Week Seventeen	. . . Thou shalt not commit adultery . . . (5:27–28)	69
Week Eighteen	And if thy right eye offend thee . . . (5:29–30)	72

Week Nineteen	*. . . Whosoever shall put away his wife . . . (5:31–32)*	76
Week Twenty	*. . . Thou shalt not forswear thyself . . . (5:33–37)*	79
Week Twenty-One	*. . . An eye for an eye . . . (5:38–42)*	82
Week Twenty-Two	*. . . Thou shalt love thy neighbor . . . (5:43–45)*	86
Week Twenty-Three	*For if ye love them which love you . . . (5:46–47)*	90
Week Twenty-Four	*Be ye perfect . . . (5:48)*	93
Week Twenty-Five	*Take heed that ye do not your alms before men . . . (6:1–4)*	96
Week Twenty-Six	*And when thou prayest . . . (6:5–8)*	99
Week Twenty-Seven	*After this manner therefore pray ye . . . (6:9)*	102
Week Twenty-Eight	*Thy kingdom come . . . (6:10)*	105
Week Twenty-Nine	*Give us this day our daily bread . . . (6:11)*	108
Week Thirty	*And forgive us our debts . . . (6:12)*	111
Week Thirty-One	*And lead us not into temptation . . . (6:13)*	114
Week Thirty-Two	*For thine is the kingdom . . . (6:13)*	117
Week Thirty-Three	*For if ye forgive men their trespasses . . . (6:14–15)*	120
Week Thirty-Four	*Moreover when ye fast . . . (6:16–18)*	124
Week Thirty-Five	*Lay not up for yourselves treasures upon earth . . . (6:19–21)*	127
Week Thirty-Six	*The light of the body is the eye . . . (6:22–23)*	130
Week Thirty-Seven	*No man can serve two masters . . . (6:24)*	133
Week Thirty-Eight	*. . . Take no thought for your life . . . (6:25–27)*	136
Week Thirty-Nine	*And why take ye thought for raiment? . . . (6:28–30)*	139
Week Forty	*Therefore take no thought . . . (6:31–32)*	143

Week Forty-One	*But seek ye first the kingdom of God . . . (6:33)*	*146*
Week Forty-Two	*Take therefore no thought for the morrow . . . (6:34)*	*150*
Week Forty-Three	*Judge not . . . (7:1–5)*	*154*
Week Forty-Four	*Give not that which is holy unto the dogs . . . (7:6)*	*157*
Week Forty-Five	*Ask, and it shall be given you . . . (7:7–8)*	*160*
Week Forty-Six	*. . . if his son ask bread . . . (7:9–11)*	*164*
Week Forty-Seven	*. . . whatsoever ye would that men should do to you . . . (7:12)*	*167*
Week Forty-Eight	*Enter ye in at the strait gate . . . (7:13–14)*	*171*
Week Forty-Nine	*Beware of false prophets . . . (7:15–20)*	*175*
Week Fifty	*Not every one that saith unto me . . . (7:21–23)*	*178*
Week Fifty-One	*. . . whosoever heareth these sayings . . . (7:24–27)*	*181*
Week Fifty-Two	*And it came to pass . . . (7:28–8:1)*	*185*

Foreword

The words that follow represent my attempt to let the Sermon on the Mount speak to me. I submit them in the hope that they may help you let the Sermon speak to you.

For years, whenever I have chanced to re-read the Sermon, I have been astonished all over again. Its novelty, force, and beauty come like messengers from a better world. Why do the world's preachers work so hard at composing new sermons, when they could read us this matchless old one? Is there anything comparable to it in all the world?

Yet for most Christians, perhaps it is true that what Jesus did matters more than what he said. And it is also true that a careful listening to the Sermon forces us to look at our lives in fresh and often uncomfortable perspectives. Still, the Sermon offers us both the challenge and the consolation of divine wisdom, distilling most of the teachings of Jesus into a single frame; we suffer a great deprivation if we miss the chance to hear it well.

As I began to read and to write these thoughts, I hoped that by listening closely to every word of the Sermon I would experience the Light that comes from that Light, and perhaps help others to experience it in their own way. It was an uncomfortable voyage, frankly, but finally an exalting one, and one I am glad I made. Each reader of the Sermon will receive its timeless truths in his or her own manner of understanding. I only hope the Light that came to me may help some others fix their own thoughts.

My wife and children and I were in the Foreign Service pursuing a diplomatic career until my retirement in 1983, so there are many references to our life abroad and particularly to our service in three communist countries, the Soviet Union in the sixties, Czechoslovakia in the seventies, and then Bulgaria, where I was ambassador from 1979 to 1981. This international experience is reflected also in the somewhat ecumenical outlook of these pages. I was reared a Baptist, attended Anglican services abroad for years, became an Episcopalian, and along the way shared in the worship of many groups, Christian and non-Christian.

My thoughts are innocent of theology or of any biblical scholarship. I am writing as a layman, for people like me who are not scholars but who wish to open their minds to what the greatest Sermon might offer them. I have used only the Authorized or King James Bible, no matter what scholars may use, since the felicity of the King James version remains unsurpassed in the English language. Its power to stir us has not diminished in three and a half centuries, any more than the power of Jesus' thoughts has diminished in nearly twenty-one centuries.

My thought at the outset of this journey up the Mount was that it would be a healthful idea to spend a whole year with the Sermon, carefully contemplating one part of it each week, thus letting it sink deeply into the mind and heart over the months. I also thought it would be helpful to my reading, and possibly to that of others, if a sentence were appended to help guide meditation, and then a short prayer added to that. But of course everyone should come to the Sermon by his or her own path, and these thoughts should be used only if they are found to be good companions.

The Sermon speaks for itself, to eternity.

Jack Perry
Charleston, South Carolina
Davidson and Chestnut Mountain, North Carolina
1984–1987

Week One
(MATTHEW 5:1–2)

And seeing the multitudes, he went up into a mountain: and when he was set, his disciples came unto him: And he opened his mouth, and taught them, saying . . .

If I had been in Galilee, that blessed day that Jesus of Nazareth said the Sermon on the Mount, no doubt I would have been too busy to go listen.

That day, I would have had sheep to tend, or a house to clean, or fields to plow, or business to see to. I would have wondered how the multitudes found time to take the day in their hands, trudge the dusty way up to the mountain and listen to this strange prophet. The news from Rome, the rumors from Jerusalem, the concerns of new taxes and old tyrannies: I would have had time for those, as usual. Yes, if I had been in Galilee that day, I would have stayed in Capernaum and kept an eye on the weather and thought about more pressing matters.

Who were they, who made up that happy multitude that went to hear the Sermon? Some were fishermen, and one a tax collector, called from their occupations by this compelling rabbi, dedicated now to following him all the way down the hard road to Gethsemane. Some were no doubt idlers and curiosity seekers, eager to hear this preacher as they had heard others, simply because he was new. But some, I like to think, were ordinary men and women trying to lead good lives, feeling a need they hoped this teacher might fill. Men and women like us, plain people, aware that their lives little reflected the glory of God, aware of a spiritual hunger at the center of their beings, laying down an hour or two in the hope of feeding on some fruit of the Spirit. Perhaps many of them said to themselves, "I have sought without finding, and my years are passing on. There is more than this. There must be a truth deeper than what I know. There must be a better world. There must be a better me."

For each of them, the day that Jesus uttered the Sermon on the Mount—like the day that he suffered on the cross, like his entire life—was an enormous meeting of time with eternity. This young Jew from the northern hills, this thirty-year-old carpenter's son, a modest member of a small nation in bondage to the great empire of Caesar: he was a part of history, treading the roads of Palestine. But more, he was eternity breaking forth into history, timelessness shattering time, Light springing from Light. For those who went to the mount that day, the bondage to time was ended as the words of Christ bathed a gray, mundane life in the sunburst of eternity. They were lifted up to a new plane of existence. They had heard the voice of God.

This year, this week, this *day*, I would like to open my ears to see if I can hear the voice of God. Despite all the noises surrounding me, the chores and bothers and cares crying out for my attention, I want to go apart; shut the world out; look for a time outside time; listen for the voice of God.

I want to close up my shop in my present-day Capernaum, take some fish and bread, put on my walking shoes, join the crowd that is going up into the hills. I want to see the Anointed One sitting on a rock against the sky, his disciples at his feet. I want to see him open his mouth as he looks down upon us, and hear his matchless teaching.

With all my heart, I want to wait expectantly on the quiet, grassy slope, and listen to what Jesus has to say to me.

Meditation: How much time do I have for eternity? Can I close up shop, walk up the mountain, and find time to listen? Can I be still and know that God is God?

Prayer: As all of the past flows into this present; as out of this present flows all of the future; here, where all that was meets all that is to be: Lord, give me grace to live in peace inside eternity. Amen.

Week Two
(MATTHEW 5:3)

Blessed are the poor in spirit: for theirs is the kingdom of heaven.

If our Lord had said nothing else, this single sentence could have opened for us the door to happiness. His words pierce the darkness of centuries, revealing a wholly new way of regarding life, its rewards, and the proper relationship of life to the divine.

This is the first of the Beatitudes, those startling definitions of happiness given us by Jesus. We have our word beatitude from the Latin, *beatus*, which may be translated as happiness. In the King James Bible, the wise translators have used the word blessed rather than happy. Blessed means happy, but it comes from a different lineage, mingling the Old English words for blood, with the idea—a crucial one for our lives—that applying sacrificial blood could sanctify, or bless, an object or a person brought to the altar of God. Blessed holds a great added dimension: the sacred is applied to the secular, and a new plane of joy is achieved.

In the Beatitudes, then, Jesus was saying, "Your life has been confined to the ordinary, the mundane, the careworn daily path. But our Father has made available to us gifts that can transform that path into something high and bright and happy. If you take into your hearts the qualities God wants you to have, then the ordinary can be replaced with the extraordinary, the routine can be supplanted by the sacred, and blessedness can transform your souls."

And the first quality our wise Savior offered to those who aspire to blessedness was the most crucial: He said we must be "poor in spirit." Surely he meant those who are paupers of the soul, who feel their own spiritual insufficiency. This is the recognition that we are incomplete, imperfect, unfulfilled, and the beginning of our hope for oneness with the divine. Jesus wanted us to be perfect, that is, completed in our union with God. The essential first thing, he said, was to reach inside and touch the hollowness there; to turn from all toward God; to be admittedly poor in spirit.

Some of Jesus' listeners that day on the Galilean mountain, one may suspect, were not willing to be poor in spirit. Life was not all that unsatisfactory; things were going well enough that disrupting it for some spiritual goal would not be worthwhile. They were the ones who listened without hearing, who went back down the mountain. But for those endowed with this longing for a larger life, Jesus said that happiness through a blood relationship with the eternal was there to be had: "For theirs is the kingdom of heaven."

In saying this, Christ was breaking the news of a revolutionary way of looking at the world. He was saying that there is another realm, inhabited by humans but not ruled by human kings, a world of freedom outside our known world of toil, suffering, and death. Many, even his own disciples, then and later, found it terribly hard to grasp this idea of a second world. To them there was only one world, and "the kingdom of heaven" meant simply the kingdom of this world ruled over by God-appointed rulers rather than the Caesars and the Pontius Pilates and the Herod Antipases. They could picture Jesus of Nazareth transfigured into a king, for the idea of god-rulers was known to them all. What they had difficulty picturing was themselves as sovereigns of their own internal kingdoms, free from the powers and dominions of the world. For when Jesus said, "The kingdom of God is within you," he meant that the person who has recognized the poverty of self-sufficiency has found the peace of heaven within.

These new definitions of happiness, of poverty of spirit, and of the kingdom of heaven—these thunder in upon our accepted canons of life. For we so readily forget that spiritual dimension of life which alone can enable us to be blessed. We forget that it is possible to establish a heavenly kingdom inside our own soul—that we must be poor in spirit before we can be rich in grace. Jesus reminds and astounds us.

Meditation: This week, I want to rediscover my own poverty of spirit; my recognition that I am imperfect, incomplete, and unfulfilled; my longing for the presence of God in my daily life.

Prayer: Father, the fraction of me that is here seeks the better part of me that is in you. Make me honest enough to know how poor in spirit I am, and lead me as I seek your kingdom inside my soul. Amen.

Week Three
(MATTHEW 5:4)

Blessed are they that mourn: for they shall be comforted.

What a strange idea, to say that the mourners are the blest, that the sorrowful are the happy! The passage of almost two thousand years has not yet yielded to most men the wisdom of Jesus' saying.

Most of his listeners on the Mount overlooking the Sea of Galilee must surely have thought Jesus was saying, "God will dry your tears." That is our first impulsive thought today when we hear the second Beatitude. I find myself instinctively recollecting Psalm 30:5.

> Weeping may endure for a night, but joy cometh in the morning.

Christ, who knew the Scriptures so well, certainly knew that psalm, and perhaps it underlay his words. But what he said went far beyond the concept that joy succeeds sorrow, that weeping turns to singing.

The old way of thinking, after all, was that the righteous, who obeyed God's laws, would receive health, happiness, and long life. Sorrows arose from sin. Hence, a return to righteousness could erase sin and restore the sinner to God's favor. But as the philosopher who gave us the Book of Job was aware, the problem of human suffering goes far beyond such clear-cut answers. Pain and death are too often inexplicable. Mourning is a part of the human condition, and mere hope for a happier tomorrow is not enough to wipe away our tears. We cry out to God not for sunshine but for answers; for relief from the despair inherent in our lives. What is at the root of that despair?

The poet-priest Gerard Manley Hopkins expressed this deeper concept of mourning most beautifully in his brilliant poem, *Spring and Fall*, written to a young child in her grief:

> Margaret, are you grieving
> Over Goldengrove unleaving?
> Leaves like the things of man, you
> With your fresh thoughts care for, can you?
> Ah! as the heart grows older
> It will come to such sights colder
> By and by, nor spare a sigh
> Though worlds of wanwood leafmeal lie;
> And yet you will weep and know why.
> Now no matter, child, the name:
> Sorrow's springs are the same.
> Nor mouth had, no nor mind, expressed
> What heart heard of, ghost guessed:
> It is the blight man was born for,
> It is Margaret you mourn for.

"Sorrow's springs are the same"—that is, they are universal—and in our rare, lonely, lucid moments we confront our own coming death, as if it were a dark figure coming down a sunset path, and we mourn. This is not a mourning that time can heal: It comes from taking a cold look at the core of human life and finding the shadow of death there.

But Jesus said, "Blessed are they that mourn, for they shall be comforted." What did he mean? No man can ever say with assurance. Some speculate that Jesus meant he himself would conquer death, so that the shadow of it would be lifted from human hearts. Some say Jesus was promising eternal life after earthly death; or that he was speaking of another kingdom, where pain and death are banished and life is blest and eternal; or that we can bury our grief in the larger life of others.

I do not presume to say definitively what Jesus meant in this deep saying. If he told his listeners that the poor in spirit possessed the kingdom of heaven, perhaps he meant that they who mourned would share in that kingdom, where comfort abounded. But that kingdom was not of this earth; it was internal, an empire of the soul. In the most direct sense, perhaps Jesus was simply saying that those courageous enough to face death would overcome it and be blest. They could say to themselves, "It is right to mourn, but there is more than mourning." Those who could accept death and pain as part of the human condition, and in accepting consecrate them upon the altar of God—perhaps they could indeed be comforted and find peace.

Living in Eastern Europe, where life is closer to the bone, my family and I found that death was a more present part of living than in our sanitized societies. In Bulgaria, where in Orthodox practice much is made of a death in the family, with recurrent religious services to mark a loved one's passing, we found the city streets constantly plastered with small death notices, paying tribute to a beloved relative who had died. In Russia, we got used to going into Orthodox churches and seeing a pine coffin sitting in the back of the church bearing a body, in wait for a funeral, with worshippers paying little notice. In our affluent countries, we try to segregate death, to put it out of our minds, to wipe out the healthful custom of mourning. We try to deny death.

Christ encompassed death in his all-encompassing arms. In this wise word he was telling us, perhaps, that life is good, but that death is part of it; that a condition of life's goodness is its sorrow; that victory over sorrow comes in accepting it; that mourning can become blessedness.

Meditation: Contemplation of the world's sorrow—including my own mortality—is the beginning of wisdom. I want to turn my eyes steadily on that true source of all mourning and, with the image of Jesus dying on a cross before me, pray for understanding, acceptance, and comfort.

Prayer: In life we are in the midst of death. Father, make me brave in my mourning. Bless me as I seek comfort in the contemplation of you. Amen.

Week Four
(MATTHEW 5:5)

Blessed are the meek: for they shall inherit the earth.

This Beatitude is alarming: Its voice is surrounded by vast silences, cutting into the heart of our established truths. Only in this savage century have we seen men openly scorn Christ's philosophy. A few critical thinkers, like Nietzsche, have dared to accuse Jesus of defending the losers of the world against the natural victors, the strong, those with a will to power. For the most part, the powerful of this world have not challenged this saying of Jesus. They have simply surrounded it with silence.

They do not accept it.

Those who possess power do not believe that the meek are blessed, or that they will inherit the earth. They believe that in this earth—despite what may be true in the kingdom of heaven—the strong inherit as they always have. And the strong are, if not blessed, at least satisfied, at least in charge. Those in power are like the ruler who asked Jesus how he might inherit eternal life, and who was "very sorrowful" when Jesus said:

> *Sell all that thou hast, and give to the poor, and thou shalt have treasure in heaven: and come and follow me* (Matthew 19:21).

The rich and the powerful do not want to hear that the way to blessedness is to be meek, to be without worldly goods, to take up one's cross and follow Jesus. That is a hard saying, and this Beatitude is a hard saying. It overturns all previous ideas of what life should be like; it was revolutionary, in the spiritual and also in the temporal sense. It was the foreshadowing of Christ's crucifixion: "Blessed are the meek."

No matter how hard I try, I find it impossible to let this Beatitude sink into my heart. I, too, surround it with silences. I try to explain it away. I say that in the world of international politics, or of national statecraft, or of business, or of journalism, Jesus' admonition was unrealistic, other-worldly. When Reinhold Niebuhr wrote the book *Moral Man and Immoral Society*, surely he was explaining that the Sermon on the Mount cannot actually be applied to international relations. When Tolstoy, Gandhi, and Martin Luther King, Jr. spoke of and practiced non-violence, actually applying the Sermon on the Mount to statecraft, they were in a pitiful minority. For the rest of us, our common sense and all our reading of history tell us that the meek suffer and lose, while the strong endure and win. How can I possibly receive this saying that the meek shall inherit the earth?

While serving at NATO Headquarters during my diplomatic career, in the mid-sixties, I had a Dutch-Jewish friend who had terrible memories of the Nazi occupation of the

Netherlands. We were having lunch in the NATO Canteen one day and were next to a table of German military officers. One had put his cap—the traditional German cap with its bill and its high peak—on the chair next to us. I noticed my friend kept looking at it. Finally he whispered, "It seems to me that every year those peaks on those caps get higher and higher." Like all European Jews, with their searching memories of the Holocaust, he could not put fear completely out of his mind. Nor should we. And against the background of horrible events like the Holocaust, we must honestly ask ourselves, "Who has listened to Jesus' words? Who *should* listen?"

Before I can answer that question, I must come to terms with another: Does Jesus really expect us to put this saying into practice? God forgive me, but so many of the truly meek people I have known, the more Christlike people, seem to have suffered the most, to have been taken advantage of the most, to have lost out on most of the good things of this life as we commonly define "good things." To turn the other cheek, to go the second mile, to give the poor my clothing, to expose myself to all the innumerable hurts of the world by being meek: does Jesus really think I am capable of this? And if I should by some miracle prove capable, why should I expect this to change anyone else's behavior? Will I not simply make room for more punishment, the more meek I become? This is indeed a hard saying.

Should I, like the certain ruler who was rich, turn away from Jesus in sorrow? Should I, like most of the powerful of history, including those in the seats of power today, surround this Beatitude with silence, and pretend it was never uttered? Or should I, God helping me, try to believe that Christ meant what he said, try to accept and to exemplify that incredible saying:

Blessed are the meek: for they shall inherit the earth.

Meditation: The question I need to face in all candor is two-fold. Can I accept the wisdom of Jesus—that the blessed are the meek—and try to live his saying and his example? And if I make that resolution, how far can I seek to apply Jesus' words to the rest of the world I am living in today? There is enough here to keep me uncomfortable for some time to come.

Prayer: Father, give me the bravery to consider my own meekness, and the grace to heed the words of your Son, that the way to inherit the earth lies in lowliness. Amen.

Week Five
(MATTHEW 5:6)

> *Blessed are they which do hunger and thirst after righteousness: for they shall be filled.*

The fourth Beatitude is like a fountain in a desert land, offering comfort in our need. These words are rich in wisdom and solace.

My personal interpretation of the word "righteousness" comes in large part from the Old Testament. Humankind is divided into those who do right and those who do wrong—the righteous and the unrighteous, or sinners. God is the very embodiment of complete righteousness. Probably my image of righteousness was formed by the familiar beginning of the first Psalm:

> Blessed is the man that walketh not in the counsel of the ungodly, nor standeth in the way of sinners, nor sitteth in the seat of the scornful.

> But his delight is in the law of the Lord; and in his law doth he meditate day and night.
>
> And he shall be like a tree planted by the rivers of water, that bringeth forth his fruit in his season; his leaf also shall not wither; and whatsoever he doeth shall prosper.
>
> The ungodly are not so: but are like the chaff which the wind driveth away.
>
> Therefore the ungodly shall not stand in the judgment, nor sinners in the congregation of the righteous.
>
> For the Lord knoweth the way of the righteous: but the way of the ungodly shall perish.

Jesus, who was imbued with the wisdom of the Scriptures, surely had this psalm in mind as he opened his sermon with the same word and the same thought. But what differences Christ brought to the word "righteous" and to his interpretation of the state of blessedness!

In the psalm, the division of the world into the righteous and the ungodly is strictly delineated. But while we sing this psalm with great admiration for the righteous, we are left with a doubt: Can we ourselves ever be worthy enough to stand in their ranks? We might wish to take our delight in the law of the Lord; but we are all too aware of our wanderings and our bent for sinning. We wonder if anybody but hypocrites can really proclaim themselves to be "righteous." We are left with doubts about our capacity for righteousness.

Jesus pierced to the heart of human weakness. His scorn for hypocrites was vehement; yet his compassion for those who struggled to be righteous was boundless. The wise Savior did not say, "Blessed are the righteous." That is what the psalmist said. Jesus knew our frailties too well for that. He said, rather, "Blessed are they which do hunger and thirst after righteousness." He did not assure us that we who aspire to be better would always attain our goals. He did say that the essential thing was to have the hunger and the thirst for self-betterment. Those with that hunger and that thirst are blessed, he said.

"They shall be filled." Their hunger and their thirst will be satisfied. Again, Jesus did not say that we would attain perfection. He knew that we would remain always imperfect, always longing after a better state and a better world. But in our longing, we would be blessed, and in our searching we would find the upward way.

In the worlds of power and of politics and of money, the kingdom of mammon, how rare it is to hear an unforced admission of shortcoming! We lived in Washington for many years, where the greatest industry is politics, and we became accustomed to parties and to politicians always claiming to be right. Little sense of fallibility here! Even less in the three communist countries in which we served as diplomats did we find any sense of guilt, shortcoming, or fallibility by those in power. In fact the Marxist-Leninist creed teaches that the Communist Party is fundamentally infallible, for it alone knows the mind of the proletariat, that is "the people." Individuals may be blamed for mistakes, but the system itself can almost never bring itself to admit errors. If there is a Chernobyl nuclear disaster, or the Soviet military forces shoot down a civilian airliner, scapegoats may be found, but we will seldom hear an admission of guilt or an apology to victims. It is a fact of history that a sense of sin is rare outside of religion.

In wiser moments however, all men see the reality of sin. We then discern that all religious thought is grounded in the idea of falling short, of sinning, of desiring to atone and to better. Wise teachers even before Christ, such as Gautama the Buddha, or some of the great Hebrew prophets, saw that man's recognition of his own imperfection—his sin, in the Judeo-Christian expression—was the beginning not only of wisdom but of spiritual rebirth. Jesus put this wisdom into the perspective of his own matchless love for humankind. He understood our frailty, our inability to attain righteousness; but he knew that our yearning to be righteous was the divine fire within us.

"Lord, wash me, and I shall be whiter than snow" (Psalm 51:7). We want to be washed of all sin, to be perfectly pure in God's sight, to be fulfilled and enlightened: to be righteous. To go on that hard path, we must witness the great suffering of mankind, see the place of sin in that suffering, and grasp the hunger for righteousness as the remedy for that sin.

Jesus did not tell us to expect righteousness, but that those who hunger and thirst after righteousness will be blessed. That is a great light in our darkness.

Meditation: If I can think about the suffering of one sick or unwanted or hungry or abused child, and multiply that by the untold suffering of mankind because of mankind's sin; if I can recognize my own share in the general ungodliness of our species; if in recognizing my sinful state I can picture myself as better, as cleaner, purer, and closer to what God would have me be; if I can yearn for righteousness: then Jesus has said that I will be fulfilled.

Prayer: Teach me to admit sin. Awaken my want for righteousness. Amen.

Week Six
(MATTHEW 5:7)

Blessed are the merciful: for they shall obtain mercy.

Having been a career diplomat, I have been fortunate in experiencing the practical ecumenism of Christianity, the oneness of the house of God. We lived in Protestant, Roman Catholic, and Orthodox countries, worshiped in all, found the hunger for God in all. Worshiping in various countries brings to life the essential unity of Christianity. It reminds us that the church draws a straight line across two thousand years of human history, years bridged easily by the laying on of hands from one generation to the next, the sharing of one generation after another in the sacraments of baptism and communion, the repeating of the same words uttered by Our Lord and his earliest followers.

Some of the earliest worship of the risen Lord was in

Greek, the language of the New Testament, and some Greek words remain to this day in the liturgies of many Christian groups. Greek words of particular resonance and holiness are the ancient, familiar ones:

> Kyrie, eleison; Christe eleison; Kyrie, eleison.
> Lord, have mercy on us; Christ, have mercy on us;
> Lord, have mercy on us.

Among the great inheritors of Christianity were the Slavs who, with the inspired teaching of Greek Saint Cyril and Methodius in the ninth century, translated the beautiful liturgy into the old Bulgarian or Slavonic that is still in use in the Slavic Orthodox churches today. In Slavonic, the words for "Lord, have mercy on us" are *Gospodi pomilui*. Anyone who has been through the solemn, ancient, and impressive masses in Russia, the Ukraine, or Bulgaria, as I was privileged to do, will never forget the words *Gospodi pomilui*, uttered or sung with such depth of feeling and meaning.

The mercy of God is thus at the heart of the Christian churches and of Christianity itself. Jesus, in this Beatitude, is telling us that we should be God-like, that we should aspire to that plenitude of mercy that we desire to see in our God.

The times of the historical Jesus were cruel. We think of Christ's crucifixion as abominable, but in fact it was typical of the cruelty of those times. Mercy was not a quality the Romans were known for. And while the Hebrew prophets had taught the world the beauty of mercy, the Jewish preoccupation with keeping to the law argued for a strict accountability, rather than lenience. The novelty of what Jesus taught is clear in one of his dialogues with Peter:

> Then came Peter to him, and said, Lord, how oft shall my brother sin against me, and I forgive him? till seven times? Jesus saith unto him, I say not unto thee, Until

seven times: but, Until seventy times seven (Matthew 18:21–22).

There was nothing in the law to limit the quality of mercy in the vision of Jesus. Teaching us to acknowledge our own sins, he also adjured us to have mercy upon the sinfulness of others. If we expect God to forgive us our trespasses, then we have to forgive the trespasses of others against us. And we should do this not in a spirit of accountability, forgiving seven offenses but not eight; we should forgive in a spirit of brotherly love, willing to forgive whatever there is to forgive.

In fact Christ was saying that we should not count offenses against us. We should let them go by, we should turn the other cheek, we should envelope offenses in love.

Nowhere is this more necessary, perhaps, than in marriage. Those whose happy marriages endure learn early on that forgiveness alone will not work. If you count offenses, and feel noble for forgiving, then the memory of offenses will grow, and some accounting must come. Those whose marriages are blessed with love learn that it is Christ's version of mercy that must prevail; the wife or husband must regard whatever comes from the partner as washed in love, and thus never to be counted as an offense.

This was, I believe, what Jesus meant when he told Peter, "Seventy times seven." If we love enough, then it is impossible to be sinned against. That is the construction of God's mercy for us, Jesus said. That is divine mercy, which we are to imitate as best we can.

That is why, down the centuries, we have prayed in our Masses and our services in all countries and places for God to have mercy on us: *Gospodi pomilui*; *Kyrie eleison*; Lord, have mercy. And Jesus always whispers to remind us: "Blessed are the merciful."

Meditation: I begin with a recognition of my own insufficiency and sinfulness. I continue with my own need for mercy. And I study my own ability to grant mercy as a measure of my worthiness to receive it.

Prayer: Grant me the mercy to have mercy. Amen.

Week Seven
(MATTHEW 5:8)

Blessed are the pure in heart; for they shall see God.

The religious literature of the world is alight with visions of what God must look like. In our mortal striving to approach the immortal, the ineffable, the indescribable, we lift ourselves to great heights of beauty and joy. Magnificent images appear in the discourses of some of the Hebrew prophets and, continuing this tradition, in the Revelation of St. John on Patmos.

No matter how grand and inspiring these may be, however, they do not bring us into the true presence of God. They are merely pale descriptions of a splendor that would be too bright for mortal eyes to bear. Our reaction is that of Moses, standing on holy ground before the burning bush: he "hid his face; for he was afraid to look upon God" (Exodus

3:6). And when Moses was actually brought face-to-face with God upon Mount Sinai, he himself was transfigured (Exodus 34:30).

Jesus had this tradition of the ineffable face of God in mind when he gave us the Sermon on the Mount. Steeped in the Hebraic tradition, he knew that mortal man did not gaze upon God or even pronounce the sacred name. But Jesus had a different concept of God. God to him was "Abba," "our Father," a figure of love. This was not a God whose name one would fear to utter, whose face one would fear to glimpse. This was the embodiment of love, whose face was the face of love, whose eyes were to be sought out even by sinful man.

Those who would see God, who would realize this most inexpressible of human desires, were the pure in heart. I would not dare attempt to define purity of heart, but surely it resembles childlikeness. The glorious thirteenth chapter of Paul's first letter to the Corinthians has always been marred, for me, by his assertion that when he became a man, he "put away childish things." (Although what Paul meant, I think, was simply that as we grow in age we should grow in grace.) I have always been attracted to those who defend childlikeness, the continued possession of what the French call *coeur d'enfant*. Marchette Chute expressed this idea well in her poem *Growing Up*:

> When I grow up I'll carry a stick and be very dignified,
> I'll have a watch that will really tick,
> My house will be tall and built of brick,
> And no one will guess that it's just a trick,
> And I'm really myself inside.

One of the most endearing glimpses into the heart of our Lord occurs when he speaks of children:

> Verily I say unto you, Except ye be converted, and become as little children, ye shall not enter into the kingdom of heaven (Matthew 18:3).

> Suffer little children, and forbid them not, to come unto me: for of such is the kingdom of heaven (Matthew 19:14).

Of all the great teachers of history—Buddha, Confucius, Mohammed, or Moses—I cannot envisage anyone but Jesus saying, "Be like children." Perhaps Jesus, in looking into human hearts, was willing to overlook a great deal that is selfish, and this was particularly true when he looked at children. Let no one say Jesus did not know sin and selfishness. But when he "called a little child unto him, and set him in the midst of them," and told his disciples to become like this child, he was surely seeing in the heart of the child the innocence, the cleanliness, and the godliness that children are capable of, and which we as adults all too often lose. This was the original of Wordsworth's celebrated picture of the happy child as father to the man, of childhood as a blessed state, trailing clouds of glory. Jesus said, if we can have hearts as clean, as pure, and as innocent as these little children, we are blessed, and we shall indeed see God.

In olden times, it was said that those with clean hearts were those who obeyed the law of God; and they were promised all the rewards of righteousness. Christ's portrait of the pure in heart was different. It was of the troubled sinner, as simple as a child searching for inward cleanliness. And those who sought such purity in heart were promised that they would come into the very presence of God. That is a lovely promise.

While living in Russia, we saw many harsh and grim things, but many happy things as well. Like most visitors to Russia, we ultimately found the Russians to be an endearing people, with very large hearts. One of their most charming features was their great love for children. We took it for granted that the grandparents—the grandmamas, with wrinkled faces and *babushka* scarves around their heads—would spoil the children utterly. But we found as well that all of the mothers and fathers doted on their children, and treated them like treasures. Loving children tenderly is to be taken, I think, as a sign of the divine spark within us.

Meditation: If the doors of my perception were cleansed, to use the words of Blake, would I be able to regain my child's heart, and to see in a child's true perspective the important and the unimportant things of this world and of eternity?

Prayer: Father, grant me a child's eyes that I might see you. Amen.

Week Eight
(MATTHEW 5:9)

Blessed are the peacemakers: for they shall be called the children of God.

A clergyman friend of mine has in his congregation a number of retired military officers. Some of them tend to have strong opinions about what has been labeled "the peace issue." One in particular—he did not come to church overly often, but he was usually in evidence for the main holidays—was outspoken as Christmas approached one year. He told my friend in firm tones, "Let's not hear any of this 'peace' business during Christmas."

Peace, a rich word, can have many meanings. The military officer had made it into a pejorative. Jesus also used the word in that sense, when he said, "Think not that I am come to send peace on earth: I come not to send peace, but a sword" (Matthew 10:34). Jesus went on to explain, on that occasion, that a true follower must value Jesus more than family, or life itself. For only in losing one's life in a higher cause can one find it. We are tempted to explain away those penetrating words in some facile way, offering different definitions of peace, as if the only interpretation was heard in the announcement of the angels at Christ's birth, "Glory to God in the highest, and on earth peace, good will toward men" (Luke 2:14). It is more compatible with the wisdom of our Lord, I believe, to accept that both peace and war are part of our world, part of our human nature.

Yet, acknowledging the reality of war as Jesus did, we must keep in mind always that he commanded Peter to put away his sword, "for all they that take the sword shall perish with the sword" (Matthew 26:52). In the Scriptures that Jesus loved there are contrasting passages. In Joel:

> Prepare war . . . Beat your plowshares into swords, and your pruninghooks into spears: let the weak say, I am strong (3:9–10).

And in identical passages in Isaiah 2 and Micah 4:

> And they shall beat their swords into plowshares, and their spears into pruninghooks: nation shall not lift up sword against nation, neither shall they learn war any more.

Can we doubt which vision Jesus cherished? He was the great apostle of peacefulness. Of all the many names applied to the Messiah, the sweetest of all, to me, is "the Prince of Peace."

Having spent my career as a diplomat, I am of course a prejudiced observer: I believe in negotiation, and in resolving conflicts among nations by words rather than by weapons. Yet I recognize that there is that in the human soul which yearns for combat, reveres the martial virtues, respects the strong. I recall the words of Robert E. Lee, on seeing a glorious charge of Confederate cavalry: "It is well that war is so terrible, or else we should love it too much." And I am familiar with the view, no doubt held by the retired military officer who wanted nothing of "peace" at Christmas, that to speak of peace and harmony among nations, to quote Isaiah and Micah, is to be soft and weak-kneed and irresolute. History is made by the strong; at least that is what men persist in believing. The diplomat, the conciliator, the peacemaker—he is unrealistic, and should get out of the way of "real men." All too often, in my experience, this view obtains in the highest counsels of government. Those who talk tough are heeded, while those who counsel patience, caution, and an attempt to reconcile differences are looked at askance. In such counsels, it would be thought an act of great folly to mention the teachings of Jesus.

And yet his voice halts us.

He tells us that peace is possible, in human history, in human breasts. He acknowledges, by listing "peacemakers" in the Beatitudes along with the meek, the mournful, and the poor in spirit, that they who seek peace are not ordinary men, and will often be subject to scorn and abuse. But he calls us to believe in a day when the kingdom of God shall be real, when nations shall not learn war any more, when love shall replace enmity, when the love of families shall extend to the whole human family. Unrealistic? Yes, of course. But Jesus challenges us to believe.

And those who believe, those who work for peace, the peacemakers, they shall be blest; and they shall be called the children of God. Remembering Christ's love of children, his calling upon us to become like children, could there be a more pleasant image than "children of God." If we lose ourselves in the imagination of Jesus, we enter a peaceable kingdom where the lion lies down with the lamb, where all of us who long for peace become children, where the Father of us all walks among us in the pastures of plenty.

Meditation: How real is the possibility of peace in the world I inhabit? Does my individual desire for peace affect the planet's possession of peace? If I want to be called a child of God, what can I do to foster peace?

Prayer: Father, we long for peace, but we have infinite excuses for war. Help us to know how relevant the kingdom of heaven is to the peace of our earthly kingdoms. Help us to find the way that leads to peace on earth, good will toward men. Amen.

Week Nine
(MATTHEW 5:10)

Blessed are they which are persecuted for righteousness' sake: for theirs is the kingdom of heaven.

The eighth Beatitude sends a troubling message across the centuries. Christ is saying—in one manner, I think—that those who dare to be different from the mass of men are blest in their difference. The herd holds to the safe pastures. Those who go off on the mountain pathways of righteousness, who, in Thoreau's fine phrase, "march to a different drummer"— they are the blest. Moreover, this marker on the road to his kingdom sends a warning: The way is beset with thorns.

Most of us do not *dare* to be pioneers; we take our comfort in being conventional. We have taken the brilliant lightning-flashes of wisdom of the great religious teachers and tamed them into organizations, rituals, ceremonies, and vain repetitions.

Most of us would have been Pharisees in good standing in Jesus' day, considering ourselves as righteous as we do today if we are members in good standing of the church we attend. But Jesus, in his unsettling message, says that not the Pharisees, not church members in good standing, are blest. The blest are the truly righteous, those who pursue a straighter path, those we often deride. And if we would be righteous, we must put our quest for the kingdom of God above our worldly quest for comfort and possessions.

Where is the divine kingdom? Jesus told us plainly:
> And when he was demanded of the Pharisees when the kingdom of God should come, he answered them and said, The kingdom of God cometh not with observation: Neither shall they say, Lo here! or, lo there! for, behold, the kingdom of God is within you (Luke 17:20–21).

Membership in the kingdom of heaven does not come with being a respectable member in First Church; or in professional success and wealth; or in titles like senator, chief executive officer, or ambassador. No, the kingdom of God is within us. Entry is gained by arduous search, dedication, and consecration, by taking up one's cross, by dying to self and to the world. And to go this road puts us, to some extent, at odds with the world. We cannot serve both God and mammon, Jesus said, and most of us would rather not hear those conscience-pricking words. To the extent that our spiritual progress rubs against our temporal comfort, we will experience, within and without ourselves, persecution.

But the reward, Jesus promises, is to discover the kingdom of heaven! That is both a startling and a heartening promise. Belonging to it is a most precious achievement, to which none of our worldly pursuits can compare; for they are all ultimately vain, while his kingdom is eternal. This is the peace that passeth understanding; this is the rest, the great solid rock that our restless spirits all seek.

But how easily are we distracted by other "kingdoms" that

also lie within—kingdoms of which the Tempter is well aware. At one time, I was the second in command at the American Embassy in Czechoslovakia. I'd been at my post only a few weeks when the ambassador left the country for a time, leaving me as "charge d'affaires," or acting ambassador in his stead. One of my duties was to represent the United States at a ceremonial opening of Parliament.

It was a typical day in Prague, misty and overcast. The romantic old cobblestoned streets of the ancient city were full of people as I was chauffeured over them in the ambassadorial limousine, the American flag flying proudly on the front right fender. As we passed, people stared at the limousine and the flag, many smiling, some applauding, and I suddenly felt full of myself, and deserving of honor. I was worldly proud.

Suddenly, however, I saw myself in another light. The car, the flag, and the office had nothing to do with my worth as a person. A feeling of shame touched me for having been puffed up with undeserved pride. I had been in a false kingdom. I had sinned.

Never again in my diplomatic career did I allow myself to feel that kind of pride again. The lesson of Jesus became real to me through my sin of pride. Those who seek righteousness, not those who seek worldly honor, have a hope of the kingdom of heaven.

Meditation: How much do I want to find the kingdom of heaven within me? Do I know what persecution is? If not, what is wrong?

Prayer: Father, none is righteous save you alone. Forgive my lack of dedication to being righteous. Make me righteous enough to deserve persecution for it. And in my journey, help me keep to the straight and troublesome path that leads to your kingdom. Amen.

Week Ten
(MATTHEW 5:11-12)

Blessed are ye, when men shall revile you, and persecute you, and shall say all manner of evil against you falsely, for my sake. Rejoice, and be exceeding glad: for great is your reward in heaven: for so persecuted they the prophets which were before you.

In this ninth and last Beatitude, Jesus warns that happiness in this world does not flow from the pursuit of goodness. The way of the world does not accommodate righteousness; men do not readily forgive. Those to whom Jesus points as examples of righteousness—the great prophets of Israel, those pioneers of the trekking soul who proclaimed justice and mercy—those good men suffered scorn and persecution. So if we would attempt to take up our cross and follow the Master, we should expect not bliss but a hard, challenging road. And we should expect, if we are serious in our quest for righteousness, to be at odds with the world.

But if we go in that way, Jesus says, we shall have a great spiritual reward: wherefore we should rejoice and be exceeding glad. I wish I were able to enter the mind of Jesus and know what vision he meant to transmit by these words. They are comforting; but I do not know if he meant that comfort should attend our road, or that we would find it only at the end. Since he said that the kingdom of God is within us, I believe Jesus meant that we would not find accommodation with the world, or success in it; but that we can find an inward peace that is more precious, more pregnant with joy, than anything that the outward world offers.

This Beatitude brings to mind the lovely hymn "Dear Lord and Father of Mankind" by John Greenleaf Whittier:

> Oh, Sabbath rest by Galilee;
> Oh, quiet of hills above;
> Where Jesus knelt to share with thee
> The silence of eternity
> Interpreted by love.

The Son of Man, on the hills of Galilee, was exposed to the hatred, scorn, and persecution of the world, and well knew where his destiny took him: to the cross. But he was at the same time the inhabitant of the kingdom of God, and in his heart was the kind of peace that he told us we could have.

During our service in Bulgaria, our daughter went to high school for a time in Thessaloniki, to which St. Paul addressed one of his letters. We were fortunate enough to visit there and other parts of the New Testament landscape. One visit that is etched on my heart is our stop at Philippi, the ancient city that saw so much Greek, Roman, and Christian history. It has been excavated, and one can wander through the well preserved ruins and picture the life of the Philippians at the time when the Apostle to the Gentiles was among them. There is even an excavated prison cell in a hillside, where it is possible St. Paul himself was imprisoned.

Visiting that cell brought to mind vividly the trials and sufferings that the early disciples and evangelists went through in following their Savior. It also brought to mind, since we were serving in a communist country, the trials and sufferings that millions of present-day Christians go through in following their faith. There in Philippi, I recalled the sadness of a Baptist pastor in Moscow who told me the law prevented him bringing his own children to church to rear them in the gospel. Since the official doctrine of the U.S.S.R. is atheism, I had seen first-hand the price he and other believers pay for their faith.

I am still trying to comprehend that, as Jesus promised, they are the ones who gain a precious peace.

Access to this peace that passeth understanding is the richest gift that can be offered. It far exceeds any earthly, secular, mundane rewards, for it is of another and more perfect world. Amid turmoil and misunderstanding how comforting to rest in the promise of Christ: "Rejoice, and be exceeding glad."

Now we have heard the Beatitudes. Jesus has offered us his definitions of the blessed state, the doors to the kingdom of heaven within us. In them, he has turned the wisdom of the ages—the ages before him and after him—on its head. He has told us that power, riches, and success in human society are not only *not* the goal, but are actually impediments to righteousness.

A. J. Liebling, that splendid journalist, has a superb passage about keeping our minds on attractive things:

> The finest thing about New York City, I think, is that it is like one of those complicated Renaissance clocks where on one level an allegorical marionette pops out to mark the day of the week, on another a skeleton Death bangs the

quarter-hour with his scythe, and on a third the Twelve Apostles do a cakewalk. The variety of the sideshow distracts one's attention from the advance of the hour hand (*The Most of A. J. Liebling*. New York: Simon and Schuster, 1963).

After all, is this not what most human activity is all about? We are the one species aware of our own future end, and the species most ingenious in entertaining ourselves so as not to think of that end. City life in all its dimensions, as Liebling goes on to say, is a marvelous distraction. Art, and music, even many human relationships—are not these also distractions? Even religion has been described as an opiate.

Jesus, in these Beatitudes, dares to look life and death in the face and to say that there is more than distraction as an answer to our mortality. He offered us an escape from the wheel of life, an exit from meaninglessness, an entry into a kingdom where God the eternal Father reigns. In the kind of prayer Jesus was suggesting, we are not to close our eyes; we are to look with level gaze into the heart of existence. We are to see that life is more than the passage of days into old age and death. Life, in the perspective of Jesus, can have meaning.

After hearing these Beatitudes, this wisdom of the ages uttered in a few sentences, we should have our eyes opened afresh and our tears dried. We have been shown the secret passage into the kingdom of heaven. The truth has been revealed to us. "Rejoice, and be exceeding glad."

Meditation: Let me ponder the Beatitudes as pathways to a kingdom of peace within me.

Prayer: Father, give me strength to let the world go, and grace to hear thy voice telling me to rejoice and be exceeding glad. Amen.

Week Eleven
(MATTHEW 5:13–16)

> *Ye are the salt of the earth: but if the salt have lost his savour, wherewith shall it be salted? it is thenceforth good for nothing, but to be cast out, and to be trodden under foot of men. Ye are the light of the world. A city that is set on a hill cannot be hid. Neither do men light a candle, and put it under a bushel, but on a candlestick; and it giveth light unto all that are in the house. Let your light so shine before men, that they may see your good works, and glorify your Father which is in heaven.*

I grew up in the 1940s and went to the Capitol View Baptist Church on a high hill overlooking Atlanta. It was a time of terrible war and then beautiful peace, and in our church, in our city, we believed that God was working his will among men. We knew that salvation was through faith, but we also believed that Christ's own people were impelled to perform those outward works that would magnify God. Since our church was on a hill, we took seriously Jesus' admonition to let our light shine before men.

I remember my father taking me one Sunday evening to the Baptist Tabernacle downtown to hear the evangelist Gipsy Smith. In his rich voice, Gipsy Smith sang "Jesus, Revealed in Me," written to a tune by E. Edwin Young:

> Oh, to reflect His grace,
> Causing the world to see
> Love that will glow
> Till others shall know
> Jesus, revealed in me.

And in the ardor of my youth, I could not conceive a lovelier way of life than to act so that those around would see always, in my light, God himself.

In the years since, I have traveled far, and have not lived up to that crystal ideal. But I can still think of no lovelier model for our lives. And I am grateful for Jesus' words, burning always inside my own darkness.

Our beautiful Savior lit lights with his words. Taking the simplest images—salt and cities on hills and candles in dark houses—he makes us see the truth inside our lives. Nowadays we take salt for granted, but we can appreciate exactly what Jesus was saying when he tells us we are salt, the essential ingredient, but that if we lose our savor—then we give nothing to the world.

But the opposite can also be true! When we find spiritual truth it will change us: We will become salt and a city set on a hill and a lighted candle.

But the essential point, Jesus tells us, is that it is not "our" light. We burn with borrowed flame: God's light.

Once again, Jesus has asked us to attempt the impossible. How can we possibly manage to be God's candles, burning with his light, making him manifest in our good works, without involving our own egos, wants, and aims? Some have done it. And the beauty of the goal is beyond all other joys.

Whenever I think of Jesus' glorious image of the candle, I think of the Orthodox churches of the Eastern world, where the burning of candles as an aid to prayer is an ancient custom. Living in Bulgaria, my wife and I used the imposing

Cathedral of Alexander Nevsky in Sofia as our "parish church," and we would often stop by for prayer. We fell into the habit of lighting candles, and found it a comfort as we offered our prayers to see hundreds of flickering candles, each representing someone's prayers.

And among the most glowing memories of our life in the Orthodox lands are the marvelous Easter midnights, when thousands of faithful stood vigil outside a cathedral in, say, Moscow, Zagorsk or Sofia, each carrying an unlit candle. At the moment the procession would emerge from the front doors with the cross lifted high, the priest would cry, "*Christos voskresye!*" (Christ has risen!) The faithful would shout joyfully in reply, "*Vo istinye voskresye!*" (He is risen indeed!) Then all candles were lit to create a beautiful impression that is indelible.

The candle still tells us, as it did in Jesus' day, that the beauty of its flame can be ours, if we can be what God wants us to be.

Meditation: Am I a candle? Have I sought the truth that can change my life? If I have found some of it, have I allowed it to work changes in my outward life? Am I willing to be a light in the darkness?

Prayer: Father, make me willing to be lit, and willing to shine before the world. Amen.

Week Twelve
(MATTHEW 5:17–18)

> *Think not that I am come to destroy the law, or the prophets: I am not come to destroy, but to fulfill. For verily I say unto you, Till heaven and earth pass, one jot or one tittle shall in no wise pass from the law, till all be fulfilled.*

One of the great blessings of a diplomatic career is that, by living in various countries where men and women become new friends and colleagues, boundaries seem to disappear and you become a citizen of the world. Diplomats can (at least in their better moments) see mankind as one. They can take as their own the fine words of the Czech educator Comenius (1592–1670) which appear on a plaque at the entrance to the International School in Stockholm:

> We are all citizens of one world. To dislike a man because he was born in another country, because he speaks a different language, or because he takes a different view on this or that subject, is a great folly. Let us have but one end in view, the welfare of humanity.

This ideal of the oneness of humankind was perhaps especially dear to me because, having been born in Atlanta in 1930, I grew up in a system of repugnant racial segregation. Seeing the South and the nation begin its rise above that evil is one of the great joys in my life. In the same way, we can see all men and women on this earth as our brothers and sisters, no less.

Strangely enough, however, many Christians who cherish this view of the brotherhood of man do not always let their toleration extend to those in other religions. Too often, we simply treat them with silence.

Jesus' love and toleration were much broader, I believe, extending to all the deep spiritual impulses of the human heart.

He was saying, I believe, that whatever the origin, whatever religion or sect, whatever jot or tittle of whatever law might be involved, the yearning for God was universal, was sacred, and was far and away the most important thing in human life.

Jesus was telling his listeners on the mountainside in Galilee: Do not separate me in your hearts and minds from the history of faith. Do not think that as a Messiah I can make irrelevant all the wisdom of the Torah and the prophets. Think rather that my divine message must include the wise and good things from the divine messages of the past. Therefore I come to bring together and to fulfill all that is good in the spiritual life of our forefathers. We need turn our backs on no one in order to turn our faces to God.

And to us today, Jesus, as I hear him, is saying: "Do not be narrow in love; be broad in love. If you love me, love all men, regardless of their faith."

Jesus assured his listeners that, until earth and heaven pass away, nothing will prevent the eventual triumph of the divine law. Taking Jesus' word "law" in its broadest sense, I believe he meant the whole body of the Law of God as opposed to, and superior to, the law of man. The surface dirt and despair is not all of it. Underneath there is a divine system at work. The kingdom of God, however far away or unreal it may seem, is the great and eternal reality. God is bringing his kingdom in, in his own way and in his own time, and of that kingdom's all-embracing love and law, no jot or tittle will pass away. This is the high vision of God's will for humanity.

Does anyone in the twentieth century have faith enough left to believe that God is working his will in our planet? Yet Jesus, speaking from the mountain in Galilee, tells us to believe that God's law will indeed prevail.

Meditation: Can I open my heart and mind to all of God's law, whatever its origin? Can I find the faith to believe that God's law will prevail?

Prayer: Father, "help Thou my unbelief." Open my heart today to every kind of truth that finds its place in your law. Amen.

Week Thirteen
(MATTHEW 5:19–20)

> *Whosoever therefore shall break one of these least commandments, and shall teach men so, he shall be called the least in the kingdom of heaven: but whosoever shall do and teach them, the same shall be called great in the kingdom of heaven. For I say unto you, That except your righteousness shall exceed the righteousness of the scribes and Pharisees, ye shall in no case enter into the kingdom of heaven.*

The first words Jesus spoke in the blessed Sermon were, "Blessed are the poor in spirit, for theirs is the kingdom of heaven." If I had been listening, I fear I would have fastened onto those first words, and would have said, "Yes, Lord, surely I am among the poor in spirit." And then I would have lost myself in thinking of my place in the kingdom of heaven. And I am afraid my concept of his heaven would have been all too close to a kingdom of this world.

Knowing our human frailties, knowing how hard it was even for his disciples to picture the true kingdom of heaven and their place in it, he instructed them about the nature of his alluring and strange kingdom. I say strange, because the first and hardest thing is to recognize that there is a kingdom of heaven. Robert Louis Stevenson's verse "Happy Thought" expresses in memorable simplicity this temptation to deny the spiritual realm:

> The world is so full of a number of things,
> I'm sure we should all be as happy as kings.

We are indeed tempted to think that all wishes can be satisfied in our diverse, teeming, and fascinating planet. Only the farsighted, or the hurt, or the poor in spirit, or the blest can bring themselves to believe in the reality of the kingdom of heaven.

When we do believe—or at least start to believe—in this heavenly kingdom, this parallel universe, we are next tempted to believe that it is like enough to our own that we can enter it by complying with the letter of God's law. Taking Jesus' reference to the divine law in its smallest sense, we take the Pharisaical way out, and say that if we abstain from the gross sins, we shall surely have a place in the kingdom.

But Jesus, Prince of Hard Words, says that Pharisaical righteousness is not sufficient for entry into the kingdom. We must go far beyond that. We must seek a broad vision of God's law, of the divine realm, and in living that vision give the example to others of the reality of the spiritual world. By saying to ourselves and to the world, "I believe," we prepare ourselves for greatness in the kingdom of God.

During my years in the Soviet Union, I was impressed deeply, to the heart, by contact with men and women of faith, whether Orthodox Christian, Catholic, Baptist, Jewish, or Moslem. Invariably, if we were in private, no secret police in evidence, and no microphones to hear, the question the Soviet citizen always wanted to ask was, "*Vy vyeruyushchyi?*" (are you a believer?). Hearing that from a Russian, knowing the depth of meaning the question bears for him, I was always a little ashamed to reply, in the facile manner of a Westerner born into a "Christian" society, "Yes, I am a believer."

The believers in the Soviet Union are closer to the kingdom of heaven than we are in the West. I do not mean their doctrine is truer, or that they are more devout. I simply mean that their righteousness has come at high cost; it has set them apart from their society, and brought them under pressures of kinds we do not experience. Their very faith has qualified them, I believe, for being called great in the kingdom of heaven. May *belief* be as vital in our lives!

Meditation: Do I believe in a kingdom of heaven that is apart from our world, and different from it, with another scale of values and demands and rewards altogether? If I do, am I prepared to acknowledge that entry into that kingdom is terribly important, but cannot be earned by the way of the Pharisee? Am I prepared to suffer for my belief in order to be a member of the kingdom?

Prayer: Lord, in praying for all those who suffer for their faith, I ask you to show me the path that leads through suffering to the kingdom of heaven, to the place in it prepared for me, and provide me with the strength necessary to make the journey. Amen.

Week Fourteen
(MATTHEW 5:21–22)

Ye have heard that it was said by them of old time, Thou shalt not kill; and whosoever shall kill shall be in danger of the judgment: But I say unto you, That whosoever is angry with his brother without a cause shall be in danger of the judgment: and whosoever shall say to his brother, Raca, shall be in danger of the council: but whosoever shall say, Thou fool, shall be in danger of hell fire.

In considering these revolutionary and disquieting words of Jesus, let us first try to put ourselves among the listeners on the Mount, and then ask our Lord to repeat his message for us of today.

Some things about the passage are evident, but other things are deeper and harder, and ultimately the passage contains a most urgent challenge to every generation.

It is evident, and surely it was evident to the Jewish audience hearing Jesus in 30 A.D., that, in illuminating God's law, Jesus was going beyond Moses and the Ten Commandments—going on to a different plane of morality. Those of old time laid down the plain rule, "Do not kill." Jesus took that law, lit it up like a great torch, and said, "Do not harbor anger or hatred in your heart. Do not *want* to kill." This is the way of love; a great revolution in thinking.

The central, profound, unsettling point was clear to anyone who had ears to hear: You may be upright, you may never commit murder or even contemplate it; but if you have anger or hatred in your heart toward your brother, you are as far away from the kingdom of God as if you had killed your brother. God is love, and you should be like God. Therefore you should love all of God's creation, and especially your fellow human beings.

Hard, rocky words. The counsel of perfection. The commandment to love all men. Impossible! we say to ourselves.

Is Jesus saying that we should love all men of all colors and all beliefs, that we should love the Shiite Moslems in Iran, those in the government of South Africa, and the communist rulers of the Soviet Union? Is he saying that governments should abstain from killing, should practice love?

We know that there have been pacifists in history, Quakers and others, who have refused to take up arms. But if we are among those responsible for government in our country, we do not see how pacifism, or unilateral disarmament, or the application of Christianity to world affairs, can possibly work. What sane man would be willing to disarm in the face of the Soviet threat? Or, our fathers would have said, in the face of the Nazi threat? Or, as Abraham Lincoln might have said, in the face of disunion and continued Southern slavery? And so on. Human nature means conflict among human groups. Surely, we say, Jesus knew this. He must have been saying, "Go on as you are accustomed to going on as far as warfare is concerned (render unto Caesar the things that are Caesar's); but in your personal life, practice non-violence and love." *Was Jesus saying that?* Or was he really telling us that if we ever hoped to escape from the age-old cycle of war and killing, we had to disarm and turn to a new way, the way of love. Is Jesus saying to our tortured century, with its tens of thousands of nuclear warheads poised for delivery at any moment, that we are indeed fools, and we are indeed in danger of hell-fire in a most literal and horrible sense? These are frightening words, and perhaps most of us are not strong enough to think on them. But Jesus said them.

Meditation: How far am I willing to go in listening to Jesus when he says that those who harbor anger toward their brothers are in danger of hell-fire? What implications of these uncomfortable words am I willing to accept? And if I reject them, what reason will I give, and how shall I square this rejection with my desire to follow Christ?

Prayer: Lord, no generation yet has proven able to follow you fully on this path of love for all mankind. Surely it is easier for our generation to wait for love in heaven, and to explain away your words on earth. I do not pretend to know exactly what you meant for me, for my country, and for all mankind to do in this matter of non-anger, of love. But I ask for enlightenment from the Holy Spirit in this very difficult matter. Help me. Amen.

Week Fifteen
(MATTHEW 5:23-24)

Therefore if thou bring thy gift to the altar, and there rememberest that thy brother hath aught against thee; Leave there thy gift before the altar, and go thy way; first be reconciled to thy brother, and then come and offer thy gift.

Religion is as broad as the human soul, and no one can encompass all of it.

I have a favorite image of religion, which is no doubt partial and small. It stems from my own weaknesses, my love of solitude and privacy, my respect for contemplation, my ardent desire to be at peace with the universe. Once at the National Gallery of Art in Washington, I saw a visiting exhibition of Chinese paintings. One, entitled "Thinking About the Tao in the Autumn Mountains," showed the solitary philosopher in his little house, nestled under the craggy mountains, peering at infinity. I was transfixed. That painting captured the mood of my personal image of what religion should do: It should free me from the petty cares of mortality, give me the peace that passeth understanding, illuminate my darkness with the light of eternity.

That kind of yearning is understandable, even desirable. It is the kind of yearning Gerard Manley Hopkins expressed in his "Heaven-Haven: A Nun Takes the Veil":

> I have desired to go where springs not fail,
> To fields where flies no sharp and sided hail,
> And a few lilies blow.
>
> And I have asked to be where no storms come,
> Where the green swell is in the havens dumb,
> And out of the swing of the sea.

But that expression of the spiritual hunger is only partial, and in the divine perspective it may even be selfish. Pietism is, after all, a retreat from the world. And Jesus, while he promised peace and rest, did not promise to remove us from the cares of this world. His kind of spirituality was the kind exercised full in the company of mankind. Preaching the Sermon on the Mount, he did not tell his listeners to leave the world; he told them to change their own hearts that they might be at peace within the world, changing it when possible, doing their duty no matter what.

In my selfish view of religion, I would like to think that if I bring my gift to the altar, to some hillside chapel or lofty cathedral or mountain shrine, that God will accept my sacrifice and give me peace. But Jesus tells me to forget about withdrawing to hillside or mountain. He reminds me that I am a man among men, that my duties cannot be separated from my obligations to society. And he adjures me to be at peace with my fellowman. That comes before the trip to the altar.

Even worse for the shy person or the lover of solitude, Jesus does not say, "What if you remember that *you* have something against your brother?" That is too easy. I may remove myself enough from meaningful society that I can successfully insulate myself from grudges and hard feelings. But Jesus said, "What if you remember that your brother has something against you?" He who tells us to be perfect in the eyes of God, also tells us to act so that men have nothing against us. Jesus' view of our duty, as his followers, was without bound or limit. There will never be an end to the demand our friends, associates, acquaintances, and even strangers put upon us. Jesus tells us to be just and righteous in dealing with everyone we meet.

A heavy burden, Lord.

It would be much more pleasant if he would let me have a general concern for the welfare of humanity, without laying upon me this obligation to do the right thing in my specific dealings with everyone I meet. It would be much easier if he would let me come to the altar, ready for his peace, without making me come with clean hands, too.

And Jesus replies, "I did not speak of an easy way. I did not promise removal from the thorns of human ties. I did not say that you could make a statement of good intent and then ignore humanity. I did not offer the altar as a refuge from life. No, I want you to remember that the test of your faith is in how you act toward your brothers and sisters. I laid upon you the burden of justice and love, a burden that is meaningless in a pietistic vacuum. I promise peace, but you must earn it, and earn it daily. But if you do as I say, and are reconciled to your brothers and sisters, and then you come to my altar—then I promise that your visit there will be very sweet."

Meditation: What must I do in my own daily life to earn the right to ask for peace at the altar of God?

Prayer: Lord, grant me the strength and the grace to love others as you would have me love. Amen.

Week Sixteen
(MATTHEW 5:25–26)

> Agree with thine adversary quickly, whiles thou art in the way with him; lest at any time the adversary deliver thee to the judge, and the judge deliver thee to the officer, and thou be cast into prison. Verily I say unto thee, Thou shalt by no means come out thence, till thou has paid the uttermost farthing.

My first thought when I read this passage, I confess, is that Jesus is not only being hard on us, he is being unfair. He does not bother with who is right, me or my adversary; he does not pretend that justice will always be done. He seems to be telling us to assume the burden of guilt, whenever there is a conflict of interests. If we do not voluntarily assume that burden, Jesus says, we may be judged guilty by those above us and, even if we are innocent, we shall pay dearly. Christians must have hearts purer than the world they live in.

Are you able to confess your own guilt and sin? I will admit that I have been hung up in this spiritual thicket. *The Book of Common Prayer* says:

> . . . We acknowledge and bewail our manifold sins and wickedness, which we from time to time most grievously have committed, by thought, word, and deed, against thy divine Majesty, provoking most justly thy wrath and indignation against us. We do earnestly repent, and are heartily sorry for these our misdoings; the remembrance of them is grievous unto us, the burden of them is intolerable. Have mercy upon us, have mercy upon us, most merciful Father. . . .

For years, I repeated those words not really acknowledging that I had done anything to provoke God's wrath. For one thing, I had read a number of wise books, like Bertrand Russell's *The Conquest of Happiness* and thoughts by Nietzsche and by the existentialists, which said that guilt was a medieval relic, encumbering man's search for well-being. The healthy-minded, post-Victorian, twentieth-century person should emancipate himself from guilt. Many wise men told me peace of mind—which in my selfish approach to things spiritual was my principal goal—was not to be found by constantly admitting guilt. Perhaps if I had been a Roman Catholic and had practiced what must be the healthy ritual of personal confession, I would have dug deeper and come face to face with my own grievous sins. But I found it easier to think about my good intentions.

Jesus is harder on us than we wish to be on ourselves. He knows that no one is without sin among us. And he tells us plainly and painfully that we are liable to pay for our sins, whether we recognize them or not. The well-being of our souls, Jesus says, is found not in explaining away our sins, or forgetting them, but in finding and correcting them. "Agree with thine adversary quickly," therefore, is a deep-cutting injunction.

If I take it to heart, and take myself by the neck and force my eyes into my own soul, I see the wrongs I have inflicted upon my loved ones, myself, and God. I see the things I might have done and the man I might have been. I see how far I have fallen short in the eyes of my Lord.

Those who would deprive us of the concept of sin endanger the essence of our humanity. The indescribable wrongs of this terrible century—the massacres of whole peoples, the camps of Stalin, the Holocaust of Hitler, the division of mankind into the rich and the deprived, the advent of horrific weapons—bear testimony to the existence of sin. That unbearable suffering of mankind weighed heavily upon the spirit of Jesus. And Jesus said, Do not pretend that you can justify yourself and escape punishment. All are guilty, for that is the nature of mankind. The only escape is to acknowledge wrongdoing.

We come, however, to the age-old dilemma of the saints among us, those who would take Christ's words literally, who would seek to abstain from all wrongdoing, all violence, all war. How can we follow that path if our adversary will not? Can I make myself clean while I live in an unclean world?

I cannot expect my adversary to be Christlike. But neither can I escape my confrontation with the words of Jesus: "Agree with thine adversary quickly, while thou art in the way with him."

Michael Bourdeaux is an Anglican priest. Since his first visit to the Soviet Union in 1959, he has made it a lifelong work to help the cause of religion behind the frontiers of the communist countries. Through his institution, Keston College in England, he propagates news from suffering believers. In one of his books, *Risen Indeed: Lessons in Faith from the USSR*, he quotes a "Prayer to Christ for Every Day" taken from a typewritten underground prayer book passed from hand to hand in Russia. The prayer is adapted from an old

Russian prayer. For me, it shines with the spirit of forgiveness that Jesus told us to adopt:

> Lord, grant me to meet with tranquility of soul all that may befall me this day. Grant that I may obey thy holy will every hour of this day; guide me and maintain me in all things, reveal to me thy will for me and those about me. Whatever news I may receive this day, grant that I may accept it with a tranquil soul and in the firm conviction of thy holy will in all things. In all my words and deeds, guide my thoughts and emotions, in all unforseen circumstances let me not forget that all these things are permitted by thee. Teach me, O Lord, to deal openly and wisely with all, in the community, in my own family . . . causing grief or embarrassment to no one, but comforting, aiding and counseling all. Lord, grant me the strength to bear the weariness of the coming day, and all the events that occur in the course of the day. Guide my will and teach me, O Lord, to pray to thee, to believe, hope, endure patiently, forgive and love. Amen.

Meditation: Can I be as forgiving as those Christians in communist countries who have so much to forgive? Who is my adversary? How have I transgressed against him? What must I do to "agree with him quickly"?

Prayer: Father, I do acknowledge my sins, I am truly sorry, and I do ask mercy. Lead me to a higher place, and deliver me from evil. Amen.

Week Seventeen
(MATTHEW 5:27–28)

> *Ye have heard that it was said by them of old time, Thou shalt not commit adultery: But I say unto you, That whosoever looketh on a woman to lust after her hath committed adultery with her already in his heart.*

The heart of what Jesus is saying is not about sexual behavior, but about the necessity of keeping our souls clean. And he is using the lessons of sex, which are of interest to everyone, to teach us a new way of looking at morals and at the life of the spirit.

Jesus had already told his listeners that he had not come to destroy the law or the prophets but to fulfill them. Now he asks them to think of that subject which always seizes our attention—sex. And he reminds them that the law says not to commit adultery, not to let the sexual drive take us beyond the sacramental bounds of marriage. But being faithful in marriage was far from enough for Jesus. As always, he was much harder on us than that. He told his Galilean listeners—

and what an astonished lot they must have been to hear *this*—that if they lusted after a woman, even in secret, even with no overt act of any sort, then they had already committed adultery in their hearts.

Now Jesus did not say, as I understand his words, that we should not have a normal interest in those of the opposite sex and their totality as human beings. Nor was he telling men not to look at women, or telling women to wear a veil, or telling us that normal regard between woman and man was wrong. He was saying that lust is wrong. And lust, as I think Jesus meant us to understand it, is the perversion of our appreciation of another person by ignoring that person's heart and soul and seeing only the person's sexual characteristics. This is a cheapening of the human personality, the reduction of a person to an object. I feel sure Jesus would have said it would be equally evil to lust after one's wife or husband if, in our own hearts, we reduce them to something less than human.

Jesus was saying, in this astounding leap into a new dimension of spirituality and ethics, that our main concern if we want to be righteous is not legalities but a clean heart. It is not for me to obey the law only, it is for me to keep the thoughts of my inmost self consecrated to God, pure and holy. I do not think Jesus was greatly concerned with normal sexual attraction between men and women. He seemed to accept the pleasurable things of life as part of God's bounty. What he wanted to tell his listeners was that there were far more important things that demanded their soul's attention. Jesus said the good life was inseparable from a good heart, a heart fixed on God.

Meditation: If I examine my heart meticulously, how much of lust and evil will I find there? Let me meditate on the possibility of a cleaner heart.

Prayer: In all the dimensions of life, give me grace to purify my heart and to act as if the spirit were more important than the flesh, the sacred more important than the profane, the lasting more important than the passing. Amen.

Week Eighteen
(MATTHEW 5:29-30)

> And if thy right eye offend thee, pluck it out, and cast it from thee: for it is profitable for thee that one of thy members should perish, and not that thy whole body should be cast into hell. And if thy right hand offend thee, cut it off, and cast it from thee: for it is profitable for thee that one of thy members should perish, and not that thy whole body should be cast into hell.

My education in the middle years of this century still reflected in great part the outlook of the Victorians. Progress was possible; the hope of a peaceful, prosperous planet was still cherished. The enormities of the war that lasted, in a real sense, from 1914 to 1945—officially, at least—had not yet persuaded us that progress backward into barbarity seemed more likely than progress forward into a higher state of civilization. We are still torn today between hope and fear, but many people have accepted the evidence of their own eyes and have begun to look at the twentieth century as a low point in man's treatment of man.

Jesus, whose own execution gave us the most deeply felt lesson of cruelty suffered by the innocent, was well aware of living in cruel times. He was surrounded throughout his public ministry by the maimed, the lame, and the suffering. He saw the beggars, the outcasts of society. He knew that the less-than-whole man had little chance of keeping himself alive, much less of maintaining any human dignity. The person without a hand or a leg in the Palestine of Jesus' day was a condemned person.

The force of these sentences in the Sermon on the Mount was thus much stronger for his Galilean listeners than it is for us today. These words brought to their minds a picture of a person condemning himself to a living death by sacrificing his wholeness. Yet this is exactly what Jesus said was the preferable course of action, rather than to be led into the paths of unrighteousness.

It is for the historians of ideas and for the theologians to talk to us about what Jesus meant by "hell." The Aramaic word Jesus presumably used, which came from the Hebrew and descended to us through Greek and Latin as "Gehenna," referred to the Valley of Hinnom outside Jerusalem, where the Israelites at one time sacrificed children to the god Moloch. It became infamous as an unclean place, where refuse was cast away, and where fires were kept burning to keep away pestilence. The word was a metaphor for a place of evil, and how exactly Jesus understood "hell" is not clear at least to me.

In my modern mind, which has difficulty envisioning a loving God sentencing souls to perpetual torture, I see the hell of Jesus as a place of darkness and evil shadows, a place marked above all by separation from the love of God through human fault and willfulness. I am not a theologian, and must apologize for venturing onto alien terrain, but that vision of hell, separation from the joys that are possible in the love of God, is a sufficient one for me.

Jesus was saying, then, in that shocking way of his, that the way of the world was not the path to the joys of God. He was saying that our will leads us astray, our own selfishness condemns us to separation from divine love. Compared to that loss, he said, what could any gain in this life mean? My eyes may be keen and beautiful, and my hands strong and skilled, but if they lead me into self-absorption, they can condemn me to hell.

So in this powerful image Jesus counseled us to ask, with knife in hand, what is truly important in our lives. If it is the wealth and the success of the world, then we risk the descent into hell, which I take to mean the cutting off of ourselves from the true meaning of life, the divine life of the spirit. I am sure Jesus did not mean to advise any of his followers to maim themselves, but that the spiritual realm is of such greater importance than the temporal that a man must be prepared to sacrifice everything temporal in order to gain spiritual wholeness and health. If that means using the knife of the spirit to cut away our spiritual unwholeness, our diseases of the soul, then so be it.

Jesus' portrayal of the dark side of the life of the spirit reminds us that many people have argued that life is happier if we exclude the idea of a spiritual dimension to it. This way of thinking leads us to assert that material things are all that is real. Although science today has gone far beyond such a simplistic view of the world, Marxist societies still contend, officially at least, that only the material world exists, that religion and a belief in the spirit are false and unscientific. The result of such an official creed, as I witnessed in my six years in communist countries, is a divorce from the deeper things of life. How can the materialist tenets of Marx comfort a husband in the death of his young wife, or a mother whose child has cancer, or the old person who has lost his or her will to live? They cannot. And so in communist countries, you will find the churches full, a religious revival underway. The drive toward righteousness that Jesus spoke of—the craving for the spiritual—remains a gnawing part of the human soul.

Meditation: Although it is an uncomfortable thing to do, I should contemplate, knife in hand, what parts of my life are unwholesome.

Prayer: Father, give me grace to sacrifice my self to the health of my soul. Amen.

Week Nineteen
(MATTHEW 5:31–32)

> It hath been said, Whosoever shall put away his wife, let him give her a writing of divorcement: But I say unto you, That whosoever shall put away his wife, saving for the cause of fornication, causeth her to commit adultery: and whosoever shall marry her that is divorced committeth adultery.

"They're better off that way" is an argument I have listened to countless times in my life. Southern segregationists used it to justify a system that deprived blacks of equal rights; Russians use it today, cast in a pseudo-Marxist form, to justify Russian rule over an empire more than half non-Russian. The rich in all too many countries use it to justify their wealth before the hungry gaze of the poor. And for centuries, men have used it to justify a subordinate status for women.

Clothing this fundamental argument in sophisticated language and logic cannot disguise its ugly skeleton: It is the rule of the strong over the weak. And the just man must ask himself the piercing question: "But what do *they* want?" If the downtrodden, ruled-over, colonized, and unequally treated are ever asked, they reply: "We want equality. We want freedom to be ourselves. We want justice."

Jesus, with his fiery sword of truth that cut through old knotty lies, saw to the heart of the matter. In the Middle Eastern social structure of his day, as in far too much of the world in our own time, a woman had a clearly inferior status. Even if she had a satisfactory role within the family, a wife was fundamentally subject to her husband. One blatant wrong was the husband's ability to divorce his wife without cause. Jesus flatly declared that this custom was wrong, unjust, and evil.

The immediate import of the words of Jesus to his first-century listeners was that marriage is sacred, binding husband and wife equally. But the still deeper import, shocking on that mountain in Galilee and shocking to those of us poring over our Bibles today, is that all men and women are truly equal. Men are not made to rule over women, Jesus was telling us: "They are *not* better off that way." Women may not be so strong as men physically, but they are as strong in soul, and they are equal in the eyes of God.

Therefore, he who would find the kingdom of heaven must include in his kingdom those whom God would include, and that means all those normally regarded as lesser, weak, and subordinate. It is often remarked that Jesus made a Samaritan the hero of a parable, giving his listeners the lesson that men of all races and creeds should be regarded as God's children. It is less often noted that Jesus, in his teachings about women, made clear that to him they were as important as men.

Our Lord sweeps away the darkness of tradition which held that women were inferior beings to be put away at men's pleasure. He gives us the image of marriage as between equal partners. Marriage is sacramental, a man and a woman becoming one flesh before God for a lifetime; not to be entered into lightly, and not to be broken lightly. Unfaithfulness, whether physical in the form of adultery or spiritual in the form of lusting in one's heart after others, is a blemish upon a sacramental relationship. Marriage is to be regarded as a sacred thing, and the most sacred thing about it is the intertwining of two human souls so that each helps the other to grow in grace. Faults and blemishes are human, and are not to be taken as causes for disregard or for separation; they are to be taken as opportunities for help, for mutual growth, for the coming together of two souls in their growth toward God.

Whether within marriage or outside of it, the status of all men and all women in Jesus' eyes was manifest: The strong should not rule over the weak; all should be under the rule of love; all are equal before God.

Meditation: I would examine my heart to see how many dark areas are left wherein I say, "They are better off that way." I should look to my own commitment to Jesus' rule of equality and justice, in whatever sphere. I should think over my attachment to what is right.

Prayer: Father, fill me with compassion for those in need of it, which is to say all of humankind. Amen.

Week Twenty
(MATTHEW 5:33–37)

Again, ye have heard that it hath been said by them of old time, Thou shalt not forswear thyself, but shalt perform unto the Lord thine oaths: But I say unto you, Swear not at all; Neither by heaven; for it is God's throne: Nor by the earth; for it is his footstool: neither by Jerusalem; for it is the city of the great King. Neither shalt thou swear by thy head, because thou canst not make one hair white or black. But let your communication be, Yea, yea; Nay, nay; for whatsoever is more than these cometh of evil.

The great urge of most of us is to complicate our lives, in the hope that within the loops and twirls of the complications we will find forgetfulness from mortality or even, perhaps, a secret doorway to immortality. But Jesus, the great simplifier, tells us not to complicate but to simplify.

I picture a pious Jew of Jesus' time, a man of good will, wanting to do the right thing, wanting to make the best of his life, sitting in the dry grass listening to this Sermon. His mental furniture includes hundreds of commandments, injunctions, and verbal formulas intended to keep him in the paths of righteousness. He has been taught that the Lord God wishes him to be a man of his word, and that by his oaths before the Lord he binds himself to righteousness. He has been taught to bind himself through complex prayers to the Lord of the heavens and the Lord of the earth and the Lord of Jerusalem and the Lord of his own life. He has been taught that if he prays correctly and often and binds himself to these great attributes of the eternal One, he will be a righteous man.

Jesus shocks him by saying this is not the way. The way to bind oneself to God, Jesus says, is simpler than that, and much harder. Forget the formulas for oaths; forget the hope of binding yourself to heaven or earth or to the Lord God himself through complicated words; forget the hope of winning favor in heaven through saying the right thing in the right way. Forget all these, Jesus says, and concentrate on cleansing your heart, mind, and soul. And to drive the point home, he says, If you are in want of salvation, and you say more than "yes" and "no," then already you are off the path.

What did Jesus leave for this listener with his eyes and mouth wide open? What did he leave for us?

This: A portrait of God in his universe that is infinitely comforting. This mighty God is beyond all our human attempts to win favor. He is a heavenly Father whose throne is the infinite heavens and whose footstool is our planet, a heavenly King who reigns in Jerusalem as in the skies. And, most comforting of all, this is a heavenly Father who cares for each of his children, who numbers the hairs on their heads, who plans their redemption.

And Jesus also left this: A portrait of ourselves, lost and seeking the right way in a hostile universe, with the inborn aim of reunion with the Father. But in this portrait Jesus cuts through all our centuries of accumulated verbiage and shows us that simplicity replaces complication, silent piety replaces public ritual, devotion to God goes beyond all expression and into the deepest secrets of the hearts. He was saying, "Do not attempt to be good in your words. Dig deeper than words, into the heart where unselfish love is found."

Jesus was saying that the simplicity of his own life was to be the great example to lead all who believed in him to eternal life—not in the rituals of faith, but in faith itself. The listener who found that faith in himself had no more need for words.

In my travels, I have been struck at how the great religions of our planet, for the most part, love to take the forthright teachings of the great founders and to complicate them enormously with ritual, rite, formula, and theology. In Japan, the complexities of the priestly rites of some Buddhist sects seemed to me in great contrast to the ultimate simplicity of Gautama's great teachings. In Yugoslavia, Greece, Bulgaria, or Russia, the proliferation of rites and repeated words in the lives of those in monasteries contrast with the simplicity of Jesus' words. So do the solemn, impressive services in our magnificent Christian cathedrals around the world. This is human nature no doubt. But Jesus still whispers across the centuries: Simplify.

Meditation: What are the complications of my life that Jesus might want me to simplify?

Prayer: Father, grant me grace to simplify my life so that I might be closer to your mighty example. Amen.

Week Twenty-One
(MATTHEW 5:38–42)

> *Ye have heard that it hath been said, An eye for an eye, and a tooth for a tooth: But I say unto you, That ye resist not evil: but whosoever shall smite thee on thy right cheek, turn to him the other also. And if any man will sue thee at the law, and take away thy coat, let him have thy cloak also. And whosoever shall compel thee to go a mile, go with him twain. Give to him that asketh thee, and from him that would borrow of thee turn not thou away.*

What astounding words! No less astounding in our ears than they were on a hillside in Galilee two thousand years ago. Mankind is still not ready to receive them.

What Jesus said was astonishing to his listeners on the Mount for two reasons. First, because he spoke of the venerable Law of Moses as being inadequate. The saying, "an eye for an eye, a tooth for a tooth," occurs several times in the Torah. These are the words of Moses, given directly to him by the Lord God on Mount Sinai, and they represent the justice of divine law. As one of the world's earliest codes of behavior, this was a tremendous advance over the primitive cruelty and chaotic injustice of prior times; and through the ages, the law of Moses had become sacred and inviolable. Jesus, a son of the Torah, dared to tell his Jewish listeners that the law of Moses was not good enough, that the truly righteous man had to go further.

Secondly, the morality Jesus imposes on us goes beyond our human conception of justice. This teaching is otherworldly; it is divine. One is reminded of Antoine de Saint-Exupery's *The Little Prince*, where the little visitor from the far-off planet, obviously a modern version of the Christ child, represents a way of life, an outlook on the universe too sweet, simple, and loving to be acceptable on our harsh planet. So did Jesus, coming from realms of light, speak to us from an outlook of eternity that we cannot comprehend, from an ethical imperative that goes beyond our powers.

What Christ said was plain enough, and one can imagine that his Aramaic was simple and direct: Do not resist evil. If a man strikes you on one cheek, turn the other. If a man seizes part of your possessions, give him the other part. If he forces you to go a mile with him, go the second mile freely. If anyone asks of you, give to him.

Plain, simple, direct. And hugely difficult.

We have spent two thousand years explaining away those words in an infinite variety of ways: "Jesus meant us to listen to the spirit, not to the words themselves; Jesus did not really mean do not resist evil, he meant that we should accommodate to certain kinds of evil; turning the cheek is a metaphor, and Jesus did not really mean that non-violence was a possible way of life; Jesus did not mean his words to apply to human groups, to churches, to nations; Jesus was not talking about my country, my armed forces, and my weapons; he was not talking about my wars. Jesus meant. . . ." and so on.

We explain away, and the words of Jesus remain before us, like whiplashes across our human compromises. We explain, and Jesus repeats his impossible words, astounding every generation anew. Occasionally, there will be those rare people—Saint Francis, Gandhi, Tolstoy, Martin Luther King, Jr.—who say, "Jesus meant exactly what he said. He meant non-violence, he meant to turn the other cheek, to go the second mile; he meant it, literally." But those people usually end up as outcasts, or are regarded as simple-minded, or as those who have retreated from the real world. Most of us continue to build alternatives around each sentence. Most of us say that these admonitions of Christ are not workable in real life. We turn the pages of history and declare that human institutions have never been able to embody these astounding injunctions. We say, in effect, "Let us worship Jesus, as the Son of God, but let us not listen to him. Let us not admit his relevance for our real world."

And above all of our defense of war, violence, and force in human affairs—above all of this, Jesus the Lord stands serene on a mountainside in Galilee, etching words upon eternity, telling us that we really should turn the other cheek. . . . We refuse to hear.

A devout Christian friend of mine who is also a fine American diplomat has wrestled with the formidable problem of trying to be loyal to Christ and to the Constitution at the same time in a professional way. A Foreign Service Officer takes an oath to defend the Constitution; the oath is not conditioned on Christian non-violence. My friend wrote, on an election eve:

> So when the voting is over and we have our newly-elected President and Congress, and state officials, let us remember that our obligation as Christians serving in government is primarily, in our public lives, to the people of the United States, all of them. The Lord Himself will bring in his Kingdom and in his time—and that Kingdom will not be America.

Yet day by day, my friend, like all of us who are both Christians and also active in public life, wrestles with the daily conundrums of conscience about how far we can go in taking Christ seriously. Certainly Jesus' words are not easier to heed today than in the time of Caesar.

Meditation: What would it mean to my life, and what would it mean to the life of the planet, if all men took Jesus' words as truth? And if all men do not take them as truth, what is my personal responsibility before those words? Should I—can I—"resist not evil"?

Prayer: Lord, give me grace to accept as much of the truth as I can bear. Amen.

Week Twenty-Two
(MATTHEW 5:43–45)

> *Ye have heard that it hath been said, Thou shalt love thy neighbor, and hate thine enemy. But I say unto you, Love your enemies, bless them that curse you, do good to them that hate you, and pray for them which despitefully use you, and persecute you; That ye may be the children of your Father which is in heaven: for he maketh his sun to rise on the evil and on the good, and sendeth rain on the just and on the unjust.*

I had been trying to think honestly about these most explosive words. I pondered them in the evening, during wakeful periods in the night, in the early morning. I wondered about the dimensions of our Lord's commandment. Was the early Christian to love the Roman persecutor? Are we in our day to love the members of the Politburo of the Soviet Communist Party? Are we to love pornographers, child abusers, those who hate liberty and pervert it? How far should our efforts go in following Jesus' command to love those that hate us? I was left with wonder at Jesus' impracticality, but with admiration of his all-embracing love.

Not long ago as I was bicycling to my office one morning, I was feeling beneficent towards the world, basking in the reflected glow of Jesus' commandment to love everyone. Suddenly, within the space of two blocks, two different drivers, a young mother with a car full of children and a young man driving a delivery truck, ran close by my bicycle and alarmed me with frightening honks of their horns. I resisted the impulse to shout at the mother, but shook my fist at the delivery truck driver. And a couple of blocks later I looked at myself and realized that my respect for Jesus' words had vanished with the honking of two horns. My heart had filled up with resentment, and I had left behind me utterly the commandment to love my enemies.

For me, this homely personal story underlines the point that human hearts, even in the very act of pondering the words of Jesus, are susceptible to an absence of love. I think of Browning's "Soliloquy in a Spanish Cloister," where amidst the atmosphere of sacred tranquility the hateful monk voices his contempt for his brother monk. All of us are susceptible.

Was Jesus telling us how perfect men should behave in an imperfect world? Or was he saying that despite all failings of the human heart, despite all the evils of this frightening world, we should strive to be full of love for all, even those who want our harm? Obviously, the latter.

Yes, the world is evil, Jesus says. Yes, you are surrounded by those who hold you and your values in contempt, those who wish to do you harm. But it is the nature of God to love all creation, to send sun and rain upon the righteous and the unrighteous. Be like God, Jesus said. Be perfect. Fill your heart with the sunlight of love for the just and the unjust. Be like the Father in heaven.

Incredible advice! Does it sound any more practical or acceptable than it did on that hillside in Galilee, even though we have been quoting these sentences for two millenia? Has anyone on this planet ever spoken more impossible, other-worldly words? "Love your enemies, do good to them that hate you"—can any of us claim to be equal to those words?

Men have found by sly experience over centuries that the only practical response to what Jesus said is to pay fond lip service and then to ignore the commandment. I admire what Jesus said, but I will put the saying aside when I am busy with Soviet missile threats, opposition politicians, rude people, and horn-honkers. I will close my ears while I go about the "practical things" of national defense, or while suing my neighbor in court and defending my rights. I will think about Jesus' words sometime in church.

But Jesus stands taller than the centuries, on a hillside in Galilee, and tells us in words that burn the heart and the conscience most bitterly, that his commandment was not meant for others, or for a later life.

In the nineteenth century and into the first years of our own, Leo Tolstoy in Russia exemplified the pilgrim who had decided, after arduous thought, to take Jesus' words seriously. A formidable intellect, a remarkable writer and man, Tolstoy inspired millions of people by his arguments for taking the Christlike road and forsaking war and armaments. He was anathema to the church of his time, and considered dangerous by the Tsarist authorities for these unworldly preachings. Certainly the communist successors to the Tsars have feared these Tolstoyan views. Yet his example remains. If you visit his ancestral estate, Yasnaya Polyana, south of Moscow in the rolling Russian countryside, you will come to the handsome old country home, and then you will go through the woods surrounding the house to the magic grove that Tolstoy often wrote about. And in it you will find his grave, above ground, unmarked, yet always covered fully and tenderly with freshly-cut evergreen boughs. It remains a spiritual experience to go there, as if it were holy ground. And Tolstoy's words about the Christlike way are still there for us to heed.

But how few of us want to hear Tolstoy, much less Jesus, when it comes to these uncomfortable truths!

"Love your enemies," Jesus says. He means it. And we still cannot believe our ears.

Meditation: If I took Jesus seriously, what would it do to my personal beliefs and actions, and what would it mean for the collective actions of Christians?

Prayer: Lord, give us fresh ears to hear the commandment to love our enemies, fresh eyes to see the need for love in our world, and fresh hands to do what you have commanded. Amen.

Week Twenty-Three
(MATTHEW 5:46–47)

For if ye love them which love you, what reward have ye? do not even the publicans the same? And if ye salute your brethren only, what do ye more than others? do not even the publican so?

Relentlessly, as his sermon progresses, Jesus is stripping away our pretensions to righteousness. We take refuge in the law, and he gives us a new law; we hide behind acceptable public morality, and he exposes our unclean hearts; we retreat to our love for our friends, surely a safe place, and Jesus implacably says that this love is far from enough: We must have love in our hearts for those that hate and oppress us; we must have love for *everyone.*

In the end, we are naked before the hurts of the world. We are brought to the admission of our inability to be what Jesus would have us to be. Still, pressing upon us, he comes again, blowing on the divine spark, telling us, to our amazement, that we should aspire to be like God.

In this dread confrontation with Jesus' high expectations, we find our defenses crumbling before his all-embracing love. If I had been at the Mount, I surely would have said, "But Lord, look into my heart and see the great love for my wife and son and daughters and mother and father; does not this powerful love mean something?"

And Jesus would say, "The hated tax collectors have that same love. Can you go no further than they do?"

In the Roman Empire of Jesus' time, the tax collectors, or publicans, were regarded as the symbol of oppression, for it was through them that the exactions of authority came to rest upon the sore-pressed men and women of Palestine. The centurion and the soldier kept order, and could be suffered as the arm of Caesar; but the publican twisted arms and cruelly exacted as much tax as he could—or so the victims felt. So that the very phrase, "sinners and publicans," was a natural one for bad people, and occurs often in the New Testament. So Jesus was saying that even the worst man has love for them that love him; it is only in going beyond this selfish love that a man becomes a son of God.

His words remind me of "Outwitted," by Edwin Markham, a little verse I read when I was young:

> He drew a circle that shut me out—
> Heretic, rebel, a thing to flout.
> But Love and I had the wit to win:
> We drew a circle that took him in.

Easy to say in a verse, terribly hard to accomplish in my life.

But Jesus did this in *his* life and in his death, as our great example. And he commanded us to do the same. To embrace the world, with all its hatred, evil, and suffering, and take it into our hearts with love. Thus Jesus presses us into the furthest corner of our defenses and commands us, "Embrace the world."

Jesus is asking us to be like him. That is a hard, hard thing to ask.

Meditation: I need to ponder the extent of my love. How much is it bounded by hatreds that Jesus would have me expunge? Do I do any better than the publicans? How wide am I prepared to spread my arms?

Prayer: More love, O Christ. Let me be capable of more love. Amen.

Week Twenty-Four
(MATTHEW 5:48)

Be ye therefore perfect, even as your Father which is in heaven is perfect.

This saying is, for me, the most sublime in the Sermon on the Mount. It is among the greatest words ever recorded. It burns; it cuts. It is beyond our understanding, yet we understand it enough to know that it challenges us to stretch out beyond our little selves. Before the divine mystery that is in these words, each of us needs to maintain silence and listen to the echoes in his or her own heart.

What follows, take as a whisper. It is what I hear when I listen to the silence after hearing these divine words.

The birds of the air praise God in their songs without knowing they are praising, and the flowers of the fields praise God unknowingly in their beauty. But we sentient human beings do not glorify God unless we will to do so. We can live dumb as stones amid celestial splendor, unless we become aware of the spiritual realm and choose to live *in* it. Alone of the beings on this planet, as far as we can tell, we have the capacity to see ourselves beside ourselves, to see the weak, shriveled, and impotent self alongside the bright, good self that God says we are capable of being.

Seeing that better self alongside, like a radiant guide in the darkness, we know that it is possible to live in both worlds, to be spirit as well as flesh, to stretch up into the ideal, to "endeavor to be what I was made," in Thoreau's fine phrase. Jesus says, "Be ye perfect." You are capable of living in the world of the spirit; you are able to attain your better self; you can become a living hymn to the glory of God—if you will.

We say, "I cannot." Or we try for a day, or for a week, and lapse into a stone-like state. We listen to Jesus' counsel of perfection, and we despair. No human being can be perfect: Is not the attempt to be perfect, then, the avenue to desperation?

> "Be ye perfect," said the Savior:
> What a crushing load to bear;
> On a path so strewn with sorrows,
> Such a load provokes despair.
> When he says, "Come rest, ye weary,"
> Then disciple would I be,
> But I dread the Savior's saying,
> "Take thy cross and follow me."

But Jesus says, "Even as your Father which is in heaven is perfect." If Jesus meant the Absolute, the End and Attainment of All Being, then his counsel would be folly. But Jesus, for one of the first times in his public ministry, spoke of "your Father which is in heaven." He spoke of "Abba," of the all-loving God who is our heavenly Father. So he was saying, Be ye love; be ye all-loving; be ye merciful; be ye good; be ye all things good, as is your loving Father in heaven. Jesus makes it appear possible to try. This was not a cruel commandment, it was a loving word of counsel from a teacher full of love.

And he did not talk about "my Father," applied to his own sonship to God; he spoke of "our Father," our common Father. This puts men and women together in society under God. He did not mean simply that we should pray a good deal, or find enlightenment by contemplating the aspects of God. He meant that we should be in the world, but not of it; we should be just and righteous in our dealings with others. In that sense he made it even more challenging when he spoke of perfection.

Ultimately, what Jesus meant was to learn to be ourselves, to the fullest extent. The Greek word in the New Testament is *teleios*, whose meaning is to reach the appointed end of development, just as the Latin word *perfectus* means "to do to the end, to do thoroughly." Perhaps other words that come near to the same exalted concept are "fulfilled," or "enlightened." But Jesus spoke to the individual within society, and his majestic words are therefore not merely spiritual, but also of this world.

He was saying, "You inhabit one world, and aspire to another: Act according to your aspirations." He was saying, "Perfection is a possible goal for men and women whose aim is to imitate God. In the striving is kinship with God." He was saying, in this alarming, inspiring sentence: "Be what you are; be like unto God."

Meditation: Let me ponder my imperfections and wonder what I was designed to be.

Prayer: Give me grace to strive always to be like you. Amen.

Week Twenty-Five
(MATTHEW 6:1-4)

> *Take heed that ye do not your alms before men, to be seen of them: otherwise ye have no reward of your Father which is in heaven. Therefore when thou doest thine alms, do not sound a trumpet before thee, as the hypocrites do in the synagogues and in the streets, that they may have glory of men. Verily I say unto you, They have their reward. But when thou doest alms, let not thy left hand know what thy right hand doeth: That thine alms may be in secret: and thy Father which seeth in secret himself shall reward thee openly.*

The idea of private piety, of confidential good deeds, is alien to our time. In Jesus' time the publicly pious made fanfare as they gave their alms. In our time those who do good, or would appear to be doing good, write books and articles, appear on television, proclaim their righteousness or their good works to the multitudes. The thought of hiding in the bosom of God and there performing our acts of worship and piety for his eyes alone is far removed from the way we think.

Do we believe in a good cause? Then let us set up a foundation, or launch a drive; and if we are seen as active in this good cause, what is the wrong in that? Do we wish to give to charity? Let us be sure we can deduct the gift from our taxes, and then let us be sure that we have our name inscribed in stone to commemorate the gift, and then let us have ample public praise as we give. Let us avoid being devoted in silence. Do we love God? Then by all means let us demonstrate it publicly.

But Jesus said that was not the way. He said that when we stretch out our right hand to give to the poor, then we should not let the left hand know what the right hand is doing. That is, we should act in perfect silence and secrecy, hidden from all men and exposed only to the all-seeing eye of God.

There may be some apparent contradiction here between this injunction to secret good deeds and Jesus' earlier counsel to let our light shine before men. But the distinction is between righteousness, the public display of devotion to God (the outward result of God's inward gift of grace), on the one hand, and charity or piety (the private expression of submission to God's will), on the other.

The good person who believes in the brotherhood of all, and who in his or her public life makes plain that commitment by acts of friendship to those of other creeds and colors: That person is letting a light shine before men. But that same person, if he or she obeys Jesus' commandment when giving help to some poor families in town, will do these alms in secret, and not before men, for in this case publicity would be for reward, and not for piety. No doubt the line is not always easy to draw. But to Jesus the distinction between the trumpet of the hypocrite and the righteousness of the good person was plain indeed. And in our hearts, we usually know as well.

I am perplexed by Jesus' promise that our Father who sees in secret will reward us openly for our hidden good works. Is a public reward what we are seeking? But this is my own shallowness that causes perplexity. In the light of Christ's wisdom, the meaning becomes clear. While we are to live in the world, our hearts are to be in the kingdom of heaven, in

God's realm. If our gaze is on him only, and we do good works as a reflection of his example, as a result of his grace, then we are blessed. And the blessing is the knowledge that in the world that matters, the world of the spirit, the supernatural realm, we have done what we should have done, not for the reward of man but for the approval of God. He offers us the peace that passes understanding, which can descend on the soul that hides its gifts in the shadows of God.

Meditation: This is a great mystery, how I shall be loyal to my faith in public but express that faith in sacrifices made in secret. I need to study the impulses of my heart, the self-serving wishes and the wishes directed to the glory of God, and to know what God would have me to do in secret and what in public. An honest, inward-looking moment can make the difference plain.

Prayer: Father, I ask that you strengthen me in faith that what I do in this world makes a difference to the working out of your will. Enlighten me as to my public duty and my duty to sacrifice before your eyes alone. Amen.

Week Twenty-Six
(MATTHEW 6:5–8)

And when thou prayest, thou shalt not be as the hypocrites are: for they love to pray standing in the synagogues and in the corners of the streets, that they may be seen of men. Verily I say unto you, They have their reward. But thou, when thou prayest, enter into thy closet, and when thou hast shut thy door, pray to thy Father which is in secret; and thy Father which seeth in secret shall reward thee openly. But when ye pray, use not vain repetitions, as the heathen do: for they think that they shall be heard for their much speaking. Be not ye therefore like unto them: for your Father knoweth what things ye have need of, before ye ask him.

A lesson in praying from Jesus is a gift beyond price.

I think the first thing he is telling us is that prayer is of extreme importance. While a graduate student at Columbia University, I heard Paul Tillich preach a sermon at chapel on the theme, "The Attitude of Prayer." His message was that the good life is, at bottom, the life spent in an attitude of prayer at all times—prayer of thankfulness, of reverence for life, and obedience to God's will—prayer that makes the moment a part of eternity. Jesus obviously saw prayer to be the center of life.

Jesus had little patience for those who used public prayer as a thing of status, a demonstration of worth, a whitewash of a soiled house. He had deep love for those who suffered for their faith. In our day, for some people, prayer brings suffering.

I remember being in Tashkent, the capital of Soviet Central Asia, and wandering only a half block off a thoroughfare. There I found in an apartment courtyard several elderly Muslim Uzbeks prostrate in their mid-day prayers. They were of one heart with the Roman Catholics I'd seen at prayer in Vilnius, the capital of Soviet-occupied Lithuania, and the Baptists at prayer in Moscow and the Orthodox Christians at prayer in many Russian towns and cities—all of them devout, all of them daring to pray in public, and all of them liable to some penalty for their faith.

But Jesus, for whom prayer stood at the center, was also careful about the uses of true prayer. Just as with alms-giving, he cautioned privacy for prayer, since the public prayer was so often for show rather than for piety.

Our Lord was also critical of "vain repetitions." I wonder what he thinks of those who repeat the Lord's Prayer publicly, all too often mindlessly? "Much speaking" is not the way to God's heart.

So Jesus' counsel on prayer is straightforward: Do not say public words so as to improve your place in society. Pray in secret. Coming together with others in worship is good, but the fundamental prayer—of which prayer during worship is only an echo—is the secret prayer of the soul seeking the divine will. That soul will not be bent on telling God things; it is the listening soul, aware that God knows needs, and takes care of them. It listens, therefore, for messages from God, and its attitude is reverent acceptance of whatever God sends. The hard part of prayer is not bending the knee, but bending the will. And the way to be, Jesus says, is as a little child.

"Pray without ceasing," said St. Paul. This was the goal in the monasteries for centuries, and still is. There life is a constant prayer. In Russia and in other lands, Christians have found a way to keep a center in their lives by using a simple prayer often, like the so-called "Jesus prayer": "Lord Jesus Christ, Son of God, have mercy on me, a sinner." Whether this is "vain repetition" I do not know, but I like to hope not. The Hindus have a saying that "the mind is like a drunken monkey," hopping constantly from subject to subject. When we try to "be still and know God" we become aware of how drunken our monkey-mind is. But the mind in tune with God will be praying always.

Meditation: What is on my mind this moment? Can I make it still, and know that God is God? Can I pray without ceasing?

Prayer: Teach me to pray. Amen.

Week Twenty-Seven
(MATTHEW 6:9)

After this manner therefore pray ye: Our Father, which art in heaven, Hallowed be thy name.

Jesus gives us the example of prayer in a glorious mystery. On the one hand, he tells us to speak in our heart, not to some ineffable distant uncomprehending image but to our Father, Abba, he who loves, in whom we can trust entirely. On the other hand, he tells us to bow in reverence before the name of God.

If we could follow Jesus' example in this glorious, mysterious combination, we would have the proper attitude of prayer and be in touch with the infinite.

We must believe, Jesus says, that in this lonely universe there is a heavenly Father who cares for all his children, including me as an individual and me as part of the society of men and women. It is the nature of this heavenly Father to love, and we are to put our hand in his, accept his love, and extend to him our utter trust.

At the same time, we must be in such awe of the Father of creation that we bless his very name, we bow before it, we express in our actions the reverence we feel for the holy name of God.

Such reverence came naturally to the Jews of Jesus' time, and we can imagine his listeners on the mount accepting his words readily. The Jews attached such great mystery and awe to the four letters which expressed the sacred name of God that they would not utter them aloud. But Jesus went well beyond this tradition. He counseled us to call God our Father and at the same time feel in our souls the most tender reverence for the name of God. He was saying, I believe, that the blessed person was the one who spends his or her life in an atmosphere of reverence for the holiness of God and for the sacredness of God's creation.

In modern times, we have come close to losing the sense of wonder, which Kenneth Grahame called "the most precious possession of mankind." William Wordsworth captured the sense of loss in "The World is Too Much With Us":

> The world is too much with us; late and soon,
> Getting and spending, we lay waste our powers:
> Little we see in Nature that is ours:
> We have given our hearts away, a sordid boon.

Oh, but I remember magical minutes when I experienced the sense of reverence for life and closeness to the heart of God! One time was staring at Niagara Falls, alone, stunned by the thunder of waters. Another was in the redwood forest north of San Francisco, awed by the uprearing of those age-old giants of the earth, feeling time slow and stop. Another was in the Alexander Nevsky Cathedral in Sofia, watching the candles burn and hearing the strong Bulgarian voices sing praises to God as the cross was carried by. Another was the Cathedral of Chartres, feeling the sunlight pouring in through the matchless windows, looking back out the seemingly tiny front door of the church like looking from heaven back onto a golden earth. Another was sitting on a hilltop overlooking the deep, cold Lake Baikal in Siberia, singing an old hymn and feeling close to God.

I could go on. But I (and I fear most of us) do not encounter such times very often. Most of our days are spent outside the temple, *pro fanum*, in profane moments that separate us from the abiding joys of the spiritual realm.

Jesus, teaching us how to pray, said that this sense of wonder, this being attuned to the beating heart of the universe, was the first commandment of the searching spirit. To sense that God is in all, behind all, pervading all. That he is a loving Father. That his realm is the realm of the spirit, holy, beyond all our profane cares and commitments. That if we are to leap into eternity, to live in the attitude of prayer, our first step must be to bow before the mystery of the universe, before the mystery of our own existence, before the greatness of God, and say, "Father, hallowed be thy name."

Meditation: Am I prepared to consider the living God as my heavenly Father, and to trust in his love, and to believe that he cares for me? Am I prepared to experience the wonder of God's universe, and to move into his kingdom by bowing in reverence before his name?

Prayer: Give me grace to be reverent before the name of God. Amen.

Week Twenty-Eight
(MATTHEW 6:10)

Thy kingdom come. Thy will be done in earth, as it is in heaven.

If God is love, and if Jesus is the Son of God, as we believe, then these two sentences give the same lofty thought in different words. The coming of God's kingdom into our world means the coming of the rule of love, the joy of the supernatural realm descended into the natural order. If obeying the will of God in heaven is the expression of universal love, then human obedience to God's will—the arrival of the kingdom of heaven on earth—will reveal itself in the outpouring of perfect love.

These pregnant sentences tell us what state we should cultivate in our souls as we bow in reverence before the name of God, as we seek his guidance in the secret hall of prayer.

Seeking God's will is the ultimate quest of the human

spirit. Men and women of all times, creeds, and races have joined the search, although all too few find the Way. The People of the Book, the Jews and the Christians, share a particular bond of deep desire in this seeking of the will of God. It is significant that out of the desert wildernesses of the Middle East have come the most eloquent, the most ardent expressions of this painful seeking after God's will.

As we recite the *Pater Noster*, how much sincerity can we put into these words, placed in our mouths by our Lord, that state our acceptance of God's will on this planet?

Did not Jesus really mean, we say to ourselves, that God's will should be done in the spiritual realm, in some special, set-aside portion of our lives, but not in the mundane world of families, children, nations, weapons, cares, egos, drives, and organizations—all of the weighty things of the real world? Did not Jesus really mean that we should recite these words, should join in them at church, should be in accordance with God's will so far as our religious devotions are concerned—but that in the rest of our lives we should obey the law and go about our business? Surely Jesus did not really mean for us to seek God's will in negotiating Tuesday's sales contract downtown! Surely he was talking about prayer life, not real life!

Charles Sheldon wrote the celebrated book, *In His Steps*, posing the question for ordinary men and women in the America of his time, "What would Jesus do?" What would Jesus do in a city neighborhood, in our day and time, facing our moral choices? One does not have to accept Sheldon's choices of the questions Jesus would ask, or the answers he would give, to admit that the query, "What would Jesus do?" is a healthy one.

In his own life, Jesus asked what was the will of God: He received a most searing answer. We can easily say that he was the Son of God, and came into the world to save sinners, and thus had to die on the cross. Yes, but he was the Son of Man as well, and he prayed that the cup might pass from him, and he asked why God had forsaken him, and his suffering as he undertook to do the will of God was suffering such as we mortals know. So we cannot take refuge from hard choices in the divinity of Jesus. Nor can we hide behind some division of the world into the part Jesus was talking about and the part he was not. At Calvary, all came together.

Therefore when Jesus told us to say, "Thy kingdom come, thy will be done," he was telling us to embark upon a most tragic search for the will of God in our lives. Try as I might, I cannot find any place to hide in those crystal, bleeding sentences. Human words find it hard to express the depth of Jesus' divine words. But he was saying, in the most literal way, that God's will should be sought and it should be obeyed.

To obey God's will for my life—what a shattering thought! If I took Jesus at his word, would I not be helping the poor, or giving all I had to the needy, or learning to care for the sick, or proclaiming the acceptable day of the Lord on the public streets, or binding the wounds of the war-torn—would I not be about my Father's business, rather than going on about my daily routine? If I took Jesus seriously, and truly asked God to let me do his will in my life, would I be where I am right now?

Meditation: If I pray sincerely for the kingdom of God to come, and for God's will to be done on this earth, what am I praying for?

Prayer: Father, give me the courage to ask you what your will is for me, and for all mankind. Amen.

Week Twenty-Nine
(MATTHEW 6:11)

Give us this day our daily bread.

I have known only a few saintly souls who were trusting enough to put their lives in God's hands.

One such was Olga, a kind and gentle woman from Guyana who lived with us and helped care for our children while we were stationed in Paris. We became friends when Olga worked for another American family in Moscow, in an apartment just across the hall from ours. "She walked with God"—that is a phrase I often think of when I think of Olga. She literally trusted in God's care, and he never seemed to fail her.

When we moved from Moscow to Paris, Olga asked to go with us. Her arrival in France is an example of her simple faith. She knew absolutely nothing about France including not a word of the language. Having gone home for vacation in South America, she was returning to Europe through London, and was to arrive at one of the Paris airports. I was to meet her. However, she was not on the flight, and I returned home in confusion.

In those days, alternate flights from London arrived at Orly and at Le Bourget airports. With one car, there was no way I could cover both. My frantic calls to both airports yielded no information. We did not know what to do, and worried that Olga might panic. We would have been even more worried had we known that she was traveling without more than a dollar in her pocketbook.

After a period of pacing our hotel room, I remembered that she had our new address in La Celle St. Cloud, a suburb ten miles outside Paris, where our new residence was sitting empty and dark since our furniture had not yet arrived. I rushed downstairs to the car, drove frantically out to La Celle, and arrived in front of our house at the moment Olga arrived in a taxicab from the airport! She could not converse with the driver, and had no money to pay him, and I have no idea what she would have done if I had not driven up. I was of course frantic, but Olga smiled her saintly smile and chided me for thinking that God might have let her down. As always, she was "walking with God."

When Jesus said, "Give us this day our daily bread," I can only suppose that he meant for us to put our trust in God for the needs of the day, without dedicating the treasure of our souls to the care of our selves. The words are not complex, and the meaning is not obscure. But the thought is too deep for most of us to accept. It goes against all the training of our adult years. And that is why Jesus, rather than telling us to put away childish things, told us to become as little children if we would enter the kingdom of heaven. He commanded us to be like Olga, to put our trust in God for our needs, literally.

Still this commandment is just as daunting as his commandment to be perfect. Who among us can truly put our trust in God to provide for our physical needs?

We have all known a few Olgas, I hope, and we know of the Saint Francises and the other glorious saints who found God in poverty, and we are aware of the tradition in the Eastern religions of going abroad with a begging bowl and nothing else, trusting entirely in the care of God. But putting our physical needs in the hands of God goes against our Western spirit. The game of life is counted in terms of money, success, and hard work well done; seeing the emptiness of all that and leaving the physical world to God is alien to us. Especially in America, we esteem winners, and look down on losers: how can we cope with the realization that Jesus was the Prince of Losers? One need not think of the extreme cases of those who ruin their lives, who actually commit suicide, in the quest for physical things; we need think only of ourselves, our absorption in the world of mammon, to see how close to impossible it is to trust God to care for us. God can care for us *after* we are secure.

The prayer of our Lord haunts us, however, if we will listen to the words as we mouth them. He suggests that we trust God to provide for our daily bread, for our physical needs. If we trust, then all of the force of our soul can be devoted to what matters in life, the things of the kingdom of God. Jesus said it was a simple matter, turning over our lives to the intentions of God. We must work very hard to complicate our lives away from the simplicity of Jesus' words. We do work hard at it, and generally we succeed. But his words remain.

Meditation: What would be the consequences for my life if I began to trust God to feed me?

Prayer: The grace to trust, Father: give me the grace to trust. Amen.

Week Thirty
(MATTHEW 6:12)

And forgive us our debts, as we forgive our debtors.

To his listeners on the mount, sitting in the bright Levantine sunshine, Jesus has said, "Be perfect." Now he tells them, when they pray, to ask their heavenly Father for forgiveness for not being perfect. And he adds, in one of those lightning flashes that send the mind of man leaping into new moral universes, that God's goodness and mercy to us should be in the same measure as our own goodness and mercy to others.

This is a phenomenal step upward in human thought, it seems to me. By being compassionate, I am responding to the compassion at the heart of creation, Jesus said. By being forgiving, by letting love show in mercy and in kindness, I am putting myself in tune with the true nature of God. If I can learn to treat others as I would be treated myself, then that very love will come back to me from the heart of God. This is a profound insight into the nature of creation, and one that still lies beyond the minds of most of us; surely beyond our normal actions. Jesus reveals to us in words, as he was later to reveal in acts, that the nature of the Almighty, the nature of God, is to be fatherly, to forgive, to show mercy, to love. And we who live in the Father's world are asked to be like him.

Not being a Bible scholar, I can only surmise, but I imagine that Jesus, in his Aramaic sentence, used a word that meant "shortcomings" or even "sins," when he used the word the King James Bible translates as "debts." Other versions, including the more familiar Prayer Book version, employ the word "trespasses." The Vulgate has "*Et dimitte nobis debita nostra*," while the French, which seems to me felicitous, has "*Et pardonne-nous nos offenses.*" Against the background of the Sermon as a whole, it seems clear that by "debts" or "trespasses" or "offenses" Jesus meant our falling short of commanded perfection in the eyes of God, our human lapses, our sins.

The divine pairing of God's forgiveness of us with our own forgiveness of our fellowman puts the whole matter of the conduct of life into a new dimension. Frankly, I can contemplate my own sins and shortcomings with some equanimity, being aware of my own good intentions, feeling that I will surely do better tomorrow than I have done today, imagining that a compassionate heavenly Father will surely see the good in my heart and overlook the shortfalls. But when I look around at my fellowman, at my co-workers, at my wife, my children, my pastor, at politicians, at businessmen with whom I deal, at all those against whom I rub in the daily friction of life—ah, then I become more vividly aware of sins, failures, and shortcomings! Then I am not so aware of good intentions, but see the dire results of sinful actions—especially when directed against me. Then I become all too inflamed at the sins of those around me.

Then as I bask in self-righteousness and in righteous indignation against a world of sinners; as I see all the ways they could do things better; as I see how sadly they have let God down; as I feel resentment against them rising in my heart, wondering if God will not find it hard to forgive this time—as all of this roils in my heart, Jesus turns his eyes of compassion upon me and says, "O Sinner, are you ready to forgive? In the measure that you are ready to forgive others, pray for a just God to forgive you."

And under that quiet gaze of Jesus, I am totally abashed. I see that my double standard, seeing the good things in me and the evil in others, does not qualify me for mercy in the eyes of God. For if men expect God to forgive all their wrongdoings and shortcomings, but are not prepared to forgive their fellowmen, how can the kingdom of God ever come on earth? In mutual love and compassion is the kingdom of heaven, where men strive to be perfect, like the Father, but where they acknowledge their debts and ask God to forgive them in the same spirit of love in which they forgive those around them. This is the peaceable kingdom. This is the fulfillment of the will of God. This is winning admission to the heart of the Father.

Meditation: As I ask God to forgive my sins, can I count on my own willingness to forgive those around me? Can I purge my heart and install the same kind of forgiveness, mercy, and love there that I would have God show to me?

Prayer: Lord, give me a forgiving heart. Amen.

Week Thirty-One
(MATTHEW 6:13)

And lead us not into temptation, but deliver us from evil.

If I try to hear the Lord's Prayer with fresh ears—no easy thing to do after years of loving repetition—I wonder if Jesus is not asking me to be uncommonly audacious before the throne of God. Am I not accusing God of leading me into sin?

No, of course not, not in the moral framework from which Jesus was speaking. Jesus was reminding us, as always, that there is a kingdom of God that we are free to inhabit, if we will—it is within us, he said. But to live in that kingdom, we must be prepared to forego the gratifications of the worldly kingdom—and those gratifications are many, real, and immediate. We must therefore say to our heavenly Father, as we withdraw to the closet of prayer every day, "This day, Father, grant me grace to live in your kingdom." By saying that, we announce to God, to ourselves, to the world, the flesh, and the devil our intention, with God's help, to abjure temptation. We declare our determination to live *that* day in the kingdom of God. Jesus did not mean us to say, "Keep me from overeating," or "Guide me away from gambling," or "Deliver me from drink," although those fleshly sins may be part of any one man or woman's worldly kingdom from which he or she must seek liberation. Jesus' view was far grander. He would have us say to the listening Father, "Help me to stay in your kingdom today."

And then, "Deliver us from evil." What did Jesus mean by evil? I can only imagine that in his supernatural mind he was speaking of evil in the largest possible way, as all that separates us from the kingdom of God. If our personal view of evil is too petty, we can never hope to find freedom from it. Jesus never said that we could be free from evil by saying certain words or obeying certain laws or rituals. No, he pronounced those fateful words, "Be ye perfect." However much we fall short of perfection, by that much are we the prisoners of evil.

If I am verily to pray, "Deliver me from evil," then I must ask myself some prickly questions. Are my intentions right, or am I inwardly hoping to use the kingdom of God as my personal path to peace of mind, to absence of care, to ease of spirit? At what point does my own piety interfere with my commitment to the welfare of my fellowman? How Jesus-like is my behavior toward those whose lives I influence—those in my family, whose days I make happy or unhappy by my attitudes and my words; those whom I work over, or alongside; those who rent from me, or owe me money; neighbors, fellow citizens; clerks and workers and all those whom I rub up against in daily life?

Other questions. To what extent am I trying to follow the

will of God in what I do with my life? Do I take refuge in my corporation, my university, or my agency, refusing to question its purposes and behavior and not daring to judge whether it is doing God's will? In my definition of evil, how far does my individual responsibility go? What about my country—do I not share responsibility for what my nation does, in a world of terrifying wars and all kinds of ungodly violence? Consider the threat of nuclear war, with its immense implications for the will of God on this planet: In my plea to avoid the kingdom of evil, should I not ask God what my responsibility is before the nuclear threat?

In uttering these simple words, "Deliver us from evil," how great a challenge we put before ourselves! And again, Jesus did not say "me," he said "us." He did not suggest that the individual can withdraw from the world and so find enlightenment. He commanded us to stay in the world and find the kingdom of God within it. He laid on us the responsibility of living as brothers and sisters with all mankind; of sharing what we have with those less fortunate; of righting wrongs done to people suffering under unjust systems; of striving for justice on earth to the extent we can achieve it, without waiting for the arrival of a new heaven and a new earth; of stretching our concept of ourselves to encompass all our powers and potential, so that falling short of the utmost would be a sin; of being what God made us to be, striving for moral perfection, attempting daily to be citizens of the kingdom of heaven. Heavy responsibilities indeed!

Meditation: Looking at myself and my share in God's world in the broadest way I can, what can I find of evil, what can I do to be delivered?

Prayer: This day, Father, grant me grace to live in your kingdom. Amen.

Week Thirty-Two
(MATTHEW 6:13)

For thine is the kingdom, and the power, and the glory, for ever. Amen.

Thus ends Christ's lesson in prayer.

What formidable syllables he has put in our mouths. What audacious attitudes he has told us to take as we speak to the heavenly Father!

We find it easy enough to repeat the words of our Lord, and we do it often enough. But if we actually think through the incredible depth of those words, how hard it is to utter them.

He tells us to go off to a secret place and to commune with God in silence, saying the difficult words under our breath. And what should we say?

We should call God our Father, daring to believe that he loves us as individuals.

We should bless the holiness of the name of God, showing heartfelt reverence for life and for all of the creation of God.

We should bind ourselves to his kingdom, asking that the divine will be done on our planet and in my own life, just as the divine will is done in the kingdom of God.

We should put ourselves totally in God's hands for our daily bread, for the needs of life, leaving those mundane concerns to him and devoting ourselves to the things of the kingdom of heaven.

We should ask God to forgive us all of our sins and shortcomings, and in the same breath ask him to show the same forgiveness and mercy to us that we are prepared to show to our fellowmen.

We should implore him to help us turn from all the manifestations of evil and to lead us to larger life in the perfect love of God's kingdom.

And finally, Jesus tells us, we should incline our heads before the majesty of the eternal, and we should humbly acknowledge that we humans have no true kingdom, no true power, no true glory, but that all true dominion, all true power, all true glory belong to God alone. *Deo soli gloria.*

In this last truth is a marvelous mystery and a great challenge.

Self-love is so much a part of our humanity that only in death can most of us merge our souls into the larger soul of God. We may say, readily enough, that we ascribe dominion, power, and glory to God; but in our inmost thoughts we put ourselves at the center of the universe, we identify our good with the good of God, we think that our piety earns us a place at the center of God's creation. The oriental religions faced up to this challenge of the littleness of man, and decreed that only in leaving our little selves could we find salvation and escape.

Jesus always saw each of us as part of the family of man. He called himself the Son of Man, and his heart was with us as brother. And he taught us, in the closing words of this matchless prayer, that only in transcending our selves, only in finding new identities in the majesty and holiness of God can we find sanity, health, and well-being.

Jesus, the Son of Man, had faced the Tempter, and knew the allure of worldliness, possession, fame, wealth, and power. He knew that the Tempter always clothes the things of this world in righteous trappings, whether the church itself, or flags, or allegiances, or dire weapons, or acts of violence, or the attainment of high standing among men. But he said, if we would find the peace of God and the path of righteousness, we must acknowledge utterly the dominion of the Almighty in our lives.

It is no easy thing to purge self of pride and to say before the visage of God that all dominion, all power, and all glory are his. It does not set easy with us. The words, perhaps, but not the admission. But it is that admission, that *sub*mission, that lies at the heart of the prayer of Jesus.

If a person were to take Jesus seriously, and send the words of the Lord's Prayer from the center of his soul into the soul of God, can we imagine what eruption of good into the universe would ensue?

Meditation: If I truly can acknowledge that all power and glory are God's, what does this imply for my ambitions and my plans? How capable am I of repeating the Lord's Prayer in sincerity?

Prayer: Give us the most precious gift, that of knowing how to pray. Amen.

Week Thirty-Three
(MATTHEW 6:14–15)

For if ye forgive men their trespasses, your heavenly Father will also forgive you: But if ye forgive not men their trespasses, neither will your Father forgive your trespasses.

If the entire Sermon on the Mount is a great bright light, then the Lord's Prayer is a brilliant flame at its very heart. Were it not so familiar, the power of its ideas would strike us dumb. Even after the passage of centuries, hearing it with fresh ears opens new vision of infinite horizons. I have read that some Bible scholars maintain that of all Jesus' words recorded in the gospels, these may be the ones closest to the precise form in which the syllables fell from his lips. It must have amazed his listeners in Galilee that day, and while some remembered some parts of the Sermon, and others remembered others, later putting the whole together into this priceless legacy, the clarity and audacity of the Lord's Prayer must have burned it into the brain of every listener. Leaving Christ's lips, it was imprinted upon eternity.

But for all that, for all our reverence before this incomparable prayer, in reading the entire Sermon we are impressed with the modesty with which Jesus presented it. He was making a series of points, after all, about the inadequacy of the teachings and customs of former times, which stressed obedience to the law rather than purity of heart; formal piety above love. In telling his listeners on the mountainside to aspire to perfection, Jesus was inculcating a new and higher law based on love. And as a practical matter, he said that the truly righteous would pray in secret and would speak to God in simple sentences from the heart. "For example," Jesus said, "something like this . . ."

And when he had finished with those supernal words, without any pause, so far as we know, he preceeded to elucidate what must have been, to him, the passage in his model prayer most in need of explanation to his Galilean listeners. That was the passage, "And forgive us our debts, as we forgive our debtors." Jesus must have thought that the rest of the prayer could be comprehended; but the originality of this thought was such that he paused to make it clearer. And with good reason. I, for one, am not sure that even with long reflection I can fully grasp the breadth of what Jesus was saying in these familiar words.

Religion had been, and for many people still is, an isolated affair between an individual and God. The expiation of sin, fundamental to all religious feeling, even the most primitive, might be a social endeavor, a collective attempt at purgation, but ultimately the effort was to obtain mercy from God. Now Jesus says, and the wonder is manifest, that God's mercy is conditioned upon our own mercy, upon our willingness to be godly and merciful in our dealings with our fellowmen. The startling insight into the nature of the divine is that the way to perfection is through learning to have a loving heart. To the extent we love, to that extent God sheds his love upon us.

Those who hold suspect the social gospel, those who seek righteousness in the context of society, should approach the Sermon on the Mount with bended knee. In this passage, which reflects the spirit of the entire Sermon, Jesus puts our relationship to God directly into the same framework as our relationship with other men. Mercy is conditioned upon mercy, forgiveness upon forgiveness, God's love upon our ability to love.

I think, with trembling, about all those in this sad and brutal world who have reason not to forgive: wives and children who are abused; religious people forced to suffer for their religious beliefs in communist countries; abjectly poor people with no hope, no future, no economic justice. These and millions more, I reflect with trembling, are also asked to forgive.

If they are asked by Jesus to forgive, can we, who are so blessed, do less? Can we close our hearts to them when we possess so much, when we are born to justice and privilege, when we are blessed with freedom? Yet how many of us find it in ourselves to open our hearts and to show compassion, love, and forgiveness for all our fellows on this piteous planet? How many of us qualify for God's mercy by exhibiting mercy to others? How many of us are willing to imitate Christ in the path of mercy, thereby earning the mercy of God?

One of the most Christlike men I ever knew was a priest who was pushed out of his parish by an unattractive minority of his congregation. Their treatment of him, after his long years of Christian service to the congregation, was shameful to onlookers. Yet the priest never said a word against those conspiring to oust him, apparently never even felt any harshness towards them. He went with perfect love and forgiveness in his heart. That is a hard way to walk, as this priest knew, as Jesus knew. I am not at all sure I could tread that path.

Meditation: How merciful am I? How broad is my personal definition of forgiveness that Jesus has asked me to show toward my fellow human beings? How much have I earned the right to ask God's mercy upon me?

Prayer: Father, forgive us, for we know not what we do. Amen.

Week Thirty-Four
(MATTHEW 6:16–18)

> *Moreover when ye fast, be not, as the hypocrites, of a sad countenance: for they disfigure their faces, that they may appear unto men to fast. Verily I say unto you, They have their reward. But thou, when thou fastest, anoint thine head, and wash thy face; That thou appear not unto men to fast, but unto thy Father which is in secret: and thy Father which seeth in secret shall reward thee openly.*

Sacraments are, in the words of the Prayer Book, "outward and visible signs of inward and spiritual grace." The history of man's religions is that the mass of people forget the inward grace, especially as the years add their accretions to the outward ceremony. Finally, the observance becomes, all too often, an empty vessel, all form and no content.

In these latter centuries, Christians have turned away from observances that impose discipline. When I was young, I heard people talk about not eating meat on Friday and about giving up consequential things for Lent; I do not know how much they were talking, and how much doing: but nowadays the idea is mostly out of fashion. When we lived in Russia and in Bulgaria, Orthodox countries, I knew many Christians who faithfully observed the old, strict dietary rules during Lent, really sacrificing for the season. And of course in the Muslim world the strict observance of the fast of Ramadan is still widespread; and very many Jews, Hindus, Buddhists, and others observe fasts of various intensities. Jesus seems to have assumed that people of spiritual inclination *would* fast—his lesson concerned how to fast, not whether to fast—and it seems to me a loss for today's Christians who do not practice this discipline for spiritual ends.

But this passage from the Sermon on the Mount goes beyond fasting, and talks to us about the very nature of religious observance. Since man is a social animal, there is naturally a social aspect to religion. Jesus made it clear that we were not only in an individual relationship to the heavenly Father, but also in a family relationship with the rest of God's children. But he was stern and hard against those who practiced only the externals of religion, those who had become so bound up in the form that they forgot the content. Jesus said that if the heart is not engaged, moving the lips and bending the knee does not matter.

Some would take this to mean that our religious practice should be bare, without ceremony. Wars have been fought over these issues. To my way of thinking, Jesus did not condemn anyone's outward practices. He went to the synagogue and joined in the services. He said he did not come to destroy the law but to fulfill it. My own understanding of the spirit of Christ is that in his loving nature he would encourage each person to take part in whatever religious ceremonies helped him be a part of the kingdom of heaven. Quaker meeting, High Mass, Baptist camp meeting, Morning Prayer, plain speaking, or candles and incense—I suspect that Jesus would smile upon them all, so long as what happens touches the heart of the participant and puts him or her within reach of the infinite.

There is the heart of the matter. Practicing the observances for their form's sake, fasting as a social gesture, church membership as a social practice, praying an habitual repetition of words, giving alms for public impression, piety as an outward manifestation without any inward feeling—all of this Jesus condemned.

The pious men of his day put on their piety like a garment when they fasted, gave alms, or prayed. Their reward, Jesus said, was their own self-satisfaction.

Those who seek more, who thirst for the approval of the heavenly Father, who seek the path to the kingdom of heaven—they would fast in secret, with face washed and head anointed. They will be in private communication with God, with no one knowing about it. Their religion finds its true expression in an inward attitude, in a secret submission to the will of God.

Those who do that, Jesus says, will be blessed—not in a feeling of self-righteousness, for in the spiritual world of Jesus one is never righteous by definition, but always aiming for godly perfection; not in the applause of their fellowmen, the feeling of shared piety; not in anything worldly.

What Jesus promises for those who seek the divine way is a lasting knowledge of failure, and the beautiful consolation of the search—the only thing that is of ultimate importance.

Meditation: How much of my spiritual life is addressed to the world around me, and how much to God?

Prayer: Father, cleanse me of my hypocritical urges, and let me seek you in secret. Amen.

Week Thirty-Five
(MATTHEW 6:19–21)

Lay not up for yourselves treasures upon earth, where moth and rust doth corrupt, and where thieves break through and steal: But lay up for yourselves treasures in heaven, where neither moth nor rust doth corrupt, and where thieves do not break through nor steal: For where your treasure is, there will your heart be also.

In this, one of the loveliest passages in the King James Bible, Jesus gives us one of his loveliest lessons. We say or sing in church on Sunday, "All things come of thee, O Lord; and of thine own have we given thee." But Jesus knew how little we are ready to give, and how hard we cling to our treasures of this world.

Life in the Foreign Service was a curious commentary upon this passage. We did not enter government service in order to make money primarily; but we were usually sad whenever we took stock after another move and found that we were once again in the hole. We found transactions in the currency of foreign countries always somewhat artificial, as if we were not spending "real" money; but this did not keep us from spending a good deal more than we had. We learned never to be "house proud"; we never owned the house we lived in because we knew we would be moving again in a short while. On the other hand, this transience made us hold the more tightly to our possessions—our furniture, rugs, pictures, books, and china—as if they could give permanence to a gypsy life. Underneath all the moving, we found that our family ties were what mattered, and what lasted; and they did not alter with the alterations of our life: They were more precious than possessions or wealth. After a Foreign Service career, we emerged without riches, but with a strong sense of family transcending geography and with some understanding that the physical treasures of this world are not the important things.

But Jesus meant us to go much farther than that. He wanted us to rise above earthly treasures of all kinds, tangible and intangible, even the fruits of talent and ambition, even—it is a hard saying—family ties. Jesus was beckoning us toward the kingdom of heaven, which was not to be entered without a leaving behind of the bright things of this world. He was saying that we could not inhabit both kingdoms, and that the kingdom of heaven was worth any earthly sacrifice to attain.

If we picture the faces of his silent listeners on the Galilean hillside that day two thousand years ago, we can easily imagine that some reflected no understanding whatever. Others may have shown a yearning to accept this teaching. But some were sorrowful, for they had wealth and did not want to lose it. They were thinking of the possessions that separated them from the poor who abounded in that day. They were thinking of what they might leave to their children. And while they were attracted by this prophet's teaching of the higher kingdom, they were sorrowful because they were not willing to give up those treasures of theirs.

And we of today? The depth of our belief in a better life after death varies considerably from person to person, no doubt, but of one thing we are convinced: the importance of possessions. Ours is a consumer society, and we are taught that what you have is the measure of what you are. Some of us care about the less advantaged in our communities and give to charity; a few of us even give contributions for the vast majority of mankind living in poverty outside our borders. But most of us manage to close our eyes to those needs, and to enjoy what we have—to salve our consciences by giving to the church and to charity, being careful to deduct those contributions from our taxes. It is the way of the world.

But Jesus said, and the words still echo, "Where your treasure is, there will your heart be also." He said that treasures are perishable. He said that spiritual treasures are the only real riches. He said that if we divest ourselves of possessions, and follow him, we can be born again into the heavenly kingdom. He said it in a loving, brotherly way. But the look of sorrow on our faces as we hear him is probably not much different from the looks of those in Galilee who heard our Lord speak. He asks a lot of us, does he not?

Meditation: If Jesus means to be taken seriously, and asks me to choose between earthly and spiritual treasures, what earthly treasures is he asking me to give up? Am I capable of it?

Prayer: Give me grace to make the sacrifices necessary to gain habitation in that kingdom of heaven which you said was within me. Amen.

Week Thirty-Six
(MATTHEW 6:22–23)

The light of the body is the eye: if therefore thine eye be single, thy whole body shall be full of light. But if thine eye be evil, thy whole body shall be full of darkness. If therefore the light that is in thee be darkness, how great is that darkness!

Living six years in three communist countries is a great education in the importance of the spiritual world.

Although life was quite different in Moscow, Prague, and Sofia, one important constant is that Marxism-Leninism is the ruling philosophy: Christianity is under an official shadow. The churches are there, but if you are a Russian, a Czech, or a Bulgarian, you pay a price for being openly religious. You are excluded from certain careers, advancement in your job might be impossible, your family is looked on with disfavor, you give up privileges. To be a success, to get your children into the best schools, to have a bit of money ahead, to be prominent in your profession—to do those things, it is essential not to be a practicing Christian.

The successful person, in those countries, falls in with the official philosophy of atheism. He or she becomes a professed materialist, scorning the spiritual life as one of superstition. And then—this is interesting—that successful person is reduced to life without any spiritual dimension. He is reduced to the shallow psuedo-moral slogans of the communist parties, to a materialist way of looking at the universe which in the tragic and moving moments of life is painfully inadequate. His eye becomes evil, and his soul is plunged into darkness.

Jesus told those listening to his Sermon that the eye of the soul has to look through the mists of this world and discern the ultimate reality of the world of the spirit. If that single eye becomes fixed on the glitter of worldly things—on possessions and the allure of ambition—if that happens then the eye of the soul becomes evil, and the soul itself is plunged into darkness.

This must have been startling to those Palestinians of 30 A.D. They had been brought up on the idea that if you obeyed the law of God, then you would have prosperity and long life. You could live in this world with riches and honor, so long as you kept the commandments, observed the rituals, did the proper praying and fasting, paid your dues to God. It was the revolutionary idea of Jesus that there is opposition between the kingdom of mammon and the kingdom of heaven, that a man must turn his back on this world in order to inherit eternal life.

Those in power in the communist countries of our century understand well that he who chooses the kingdom of God, as Jesus commanded his followers to do, must necessarily turn away from the kingdoms of this earth. Dual loyalty is not possible, in the ultimate sense, according to the words of Jesus.

We squirm and compromise, of course. Many, many dwellers in communist lands manage to live a respectable life in the sense of currying favor within the communist system, consoling themselves with prayer and with an occasional visit to a church. But we dwellers in freer countries should not look at the speck in their eye. In our own lives, we manage all too often to pretend that the kingdom of heaven incorporates all of the good things of life, so that we can live comfortably with feet in both camps. Surely Jesus did not mean for us to lower our standard of living. Surely we must get along in this world while we prepare for the next!

But Jesus was the great *un*compromiser. He did not suggest some halfway accommodation. Jesus said that the man or woman who seeks the kingdom of heaven, who believes in the essentiality of the spiritual world—that person has a single, whole, healthy eye, a seeing eye of the soul. And with that good eye, the flooding of the spirit can come in, so that the whole body will be full of light.

My heart goes out to those in communist countries who must make the hard choice between the wholehearted practice of their faith and the welfare of their families and children. God help them on their stony path. But my heart also goes out to those of us living in freedom, who face Jesus' challenge to choose between mammon and God. I wonder how many who heard the Sermon on the Mount took up that challenge. I wonder how many do today.

Meditation: What shall I see with the single eye of my soul, darkness or light?

Prayer: Father, give me grace to have a single eye so that my whole body might be full of light. Amen.

Week Thirty-Seven
(MATTHEW 6:24)

No man can serve two masters: for either he will hate the one, and love the other; or else he will hold to the one and despise the other. Ye cannot serve God and mammon.

When I was between fifteen and twenty-five, that difficult decade when all the joys and sorrows of life crowd in upon you with almost unbearable intensity, I could not understand why people did not take Jesus more seriously. In my innocence, I said to myself, "If they truly believe, why do they not listen to the words of Jesus, and put aside false gods and follow the master?" I read about other religions, and saw beauty in all of them, and always wondered why men of today ignored the wisdom of the ages.

As I grew older, I saw, of course, that to cherish the divine words was not the same as putting them into practice. Indeed the spirit is willing but the flesh is weak. It is not that we do not believe, exactly, but the practicalities of life—

mammon, Jesus called it; the bondage of aimless action, in the words of the *Bhagavad Gita*—crowd out our higher intentions, and most of us forget our quest for the kingdom.

Jesus did not tell us that it would be easy, at any age. He used an Aramaic word, *mamona*, which then entered into Greek and Latin and on down into English and other languages, from his usage; and if the word originally meant "riches," Jesus put into it, in the Sermon on the Mount, all the broad meaning of The Things of This World. Jesus knew how hard it is to turn our backs on those things. The rich, young ruler went away sorrowing, because Jesus told him to give all he had to the poor and to follow him. Jesus sorrowed as well, saying, "How hardly shall they that have riches enter into the kingdom of God" (Luke 18:24).

Do you suppose that I was wiser when I was sixteen than I am today, some forty years later? Are we, in our youth, still trailing clouds of glory, closer to heaven, not yet corrupted by the good things of this earth? If Jesus uttered these sayings on the Mount towards the beginning of his ministry, as we suppose, he was according to most scholars around thirty years old. This was, for New Testament times, a respectable age, certainly not a time of youth. When Jesus called his disciples, they were mature men, not old, but men already in callings. He said those who want to enter the kingdom of heaven should become as children; he said this to grown-up men and women, those who already had possessions, who were part of this world, who knew mammon first hand. He spoke in Aramaic to Galileans, but he meant his message for us, for today.

And Jesus said, in the plainest words, that if we wish to enter the kingdom of God, we have to choose it, and in choosing we have to leave the kingdom of mammon. "No man can serve two masters." Uncomfortable words. We can explain them away: Jesus must have meant that we should put spiritual things first, while pursuing our necessary ends in the material world.

But like a bell that rang two thousand years ago and whose pure tones continue to sound over the centuries, the words of Jesus penetrate our ears and our hearts. The message is that there are two kingdoms: one of this world, of riches, of mammon; the other of God. Dual citizenship, Jesus said, does not exist for these two kingdoms. We must choose.

And turning one's back on the kingdom of this earth is as difficult for us today as it was for that rich ruler. To withdraw from this world, and to seek admission to the kingdom of God, is the hardest thing to do. Jesus did not say his way was easy.

Meditation: In my life, what is mammon?

Prayer: (From the *Sarum Primer*)

> God be in my head, and in my understanding;
> God be in my eyes, and in my looking;
> God be in my mouth, and in my speaking;
> God be in my heart, and in my thinking;
> God be at my end, and at my departing.

Week Thirty-Eight
(MATTHEW 6:25–27)

> *Therefore I say unto you, Take no thought for your life, what ye shall eat, or what ye shall drink; nor yet for your body, what ye shall put on. Is not the life more than meat, and the body than raiment? Behold the fowls of the air: for they sow not, neither do they reap, nor gather into barns; yet your heavenly Father feedeth them. Are ye not much better than they? Which of you by taking thought can add one cubit unto his stature?*

The blessed minority in any age are those who divide the important from the unimportant, who see to the heart of things, who dwell in eternity.

The wisdom of the East is rich in the lore of those who perceived the transience of this world, those who attained enlightenment by grasping hold of the lasting. But only the wisest of men throughout the ages have taken hold of this truth. No one, to my way of thinking, has expressed it more beautifully than Jesus. Pointing to the birds as the images of God's grace, creatures blessed by the Father in voice and in flight, Jesus told us that if we but had faith, we should be freer than the flight of the birds, we should have songs in our hearts sweeter than the song of the birds.

Do you know anyone who believes it? Who acts as if he believes it? Are not all of us on this crowded planet preoccupied with meat and raiment, getting and spending, trying in vain to add cubits to our stature?

My heart goes out to those living in communist countries, for their official philosophy is materialism, and the people are taught that more possessions, more things, means happiness. The contrast between the promise and the emptiness of real life is sobering.

My heart goes out as well to those living in the poor countries, those with scant chance in their lifetime of having the minimum needed for a comfortable life. Had they renounced riches voluntarily, perhaps they might be happy, but the man born to poverty finds it hard to be wise; his thoughts are naturally fixed on those material things he does not have.

And my heart goes out, above all, to those of us living in the affluent West, where a philosophy of consumerism reigns, where we are taught that a growing economy with more and more products for everyone to consume is the equivalent of the good life. The ultimate emptiness of that philosophy is apparent in Jesus' reference to the birds.

When we were serving at the American Embassy in Moscow, an American student friend of ours at Moscow University told us about a long conversation some American and Russian students had about what life would be like in the Soviet Union when "communism was attained"—that future stage when socialism is fulfilled, when, according to Marxism, the good life will be reached. Bound up in their materialist philosophy, the Russian students' description of that ideal life sounded more and more familiar to the Americans, accustomed as they were to a consumer society. Finally one of the

Americans said, "But what you are describing is California today!"

The aim of mankind in our century seems fixed: as many material possessions as possible.

Jesus said that this was not the way to the kingdom of heaven. He said material possessions are encumbrances, preventing us from seeking union with God. The wise man, the good man, the righteous man, hungers and thirsts after righteousness, not after mammon. Jesus said that his followers should forget trying to add inches to their height, or trying to have delicious things to eat, or beautiful clothes to wear. We should regard the birds of the air, singing halfway to heaven, and let them be our models.

Jesus said that if we turn our eyes away from the riches of this world, and put ourselves into the hands of our heavenly Father, then this world will take care of itself, and we can invest the riches of our soul in the kingdom of heaven.

We can be utterly free, if we would only let the world go.

Meditation: What if I should practice peeling away my attractions, desires, and wants, one by one, like the leaves of an artichoke, until I should come, finally, to the heart of the matter, the love of God?

Prayer: Father, give me the wings of the birds that I might rise above my love of the things of this world. Amen.

Week Thirty-Nine
(MATTHEW 6:28–30)

And why take ye thought for raiment? Consider the lilies of the field, how they grow; they toil not, neither do they spin: And yet I say unto you, That even Solomon in all his glory was not arrayed like one of these. Wherefore, if God so clothe the grass of the field, which today is, and tomorrow is cast into the oven, shall he not much more clothe you, O ye of little faith?

O we of little faith! How hard it is for us to live free within the wonder and the beauty of God's creation. We fail to open our eyes.

Our wise Savior said many words revealing the nature of God, and of man, and of his own blessed mind. This one little story, as brilliant as a sunbeam, lights up a precious corner of the divine nature, showing us Jesus the Poet. What a lovely thing to do, in the middle of this Sermon of uncomfortable truths, to pause, and to point to a wildflower—may we not imagine Jesus of Nazareth stooping to cup the lily, framing the lesson in his own dear hand?—and to say that the great king himself could not rival the glory of this frail blossom. It is a sweet conceit, and worthy of a great poet. It shows us that our Savior was alive to the beauties of this earth.

Vita brevis, ars longa, it is said, and "a thing of beauty is a joy forever." In the decay and impermanence of human life, all people of sensitivity are aware of *lacrimae rerum,* the pathos within things. That awareness leads to tears. It also leads to a human hunger for permanence, for holding on to the lasting things. Objects of beauty, whether in nature or in the higher creations of man, satisfy this hunger. When Jesus made his listeners know that the humble lily of the field was more glorious that all the glory of King Solomon himself, then he was reminding them that beauty can help relieve our human sorrow.

But Jesus went deeper, seeing that beauty is merely an aspect of the glory of God. The highest beauty is the "beauty of holiness," and it is within that beauty that we should worship God and trust in him completely. As the world enfolds us—just as it enfolded those men and women on the mount—Jesus would have us turn our eyes in faith to the author of all beauty, and be aware of his unchanging nature. Gerard Manley Hopkins told it beautifully in "God's Grandeur":

> The world is charged with the grandeur of God.
> It will flame out, like shining from shook foil;
> It gathers to a greatness, like the ooze of oil
> Crushed. Why do men then now not reck his rod?
> Generations have trod, have trod, have trod;
> And all is seared with trade; bleared, smeared with toil;
> And wears man's smudge and shares man's smell: the soil
> Is bare now, nor can foot feel, being shod.
>
> And for all this, nature is never spent;
> There lives the dearest freshness deep down things;
> And though the last lights off the black West went

Oh, morning, at the brown brink eastward, springs—
Because the Holy Ghost over the bent
World broods with warm breast and with ah! bright wings.

I do not doubt that if our faith were as large as Jesus told us it should be, we should walk in wonder in this earth and be aware of the lilies out-glorying Solomon, sense the Holy Ghost brooding over our world with bright wings, and see the grandeur of God flaming out of a beauty-charged universe. But we are of little faith.

When I am on trips—and trips are valuable, taking us up out of the prisons of our daily routines—I sometimes find myself looking at the sky with open eyes and closed mind. If I am driving, I may be listening to Mozart or contemplating a talk I must give, but my eyes take in the road and nothing else. Or if I am flying, I am reading, or looking at the seat in front of me, without opening my inward eyes. Then moments come—who knows why?—when I open the door to my mind and see the immensity and the beauty of the clouds towering into the eternal blue of the sky. I am shaken, moved sometimes to the point of tears. The wonder of the world to which I have been blind has suddenly come home to me.

Listening to the blessed words of Jesus in the Sermon, I am persuaded that he would have us keep our eyes open at all times. He would have us look at the lilies of the field all around us, the clouds in their eternal sky, and see the glory of God. And more, he would have us see in this beauty the reassurance that God loves us and will care for us down to the edge of the world, down through the doors of death itself. If God creates the unfathomable, mysterious beauty of this wild lily, the Savior says, and sustains it with rain and sunshine, will God not sustain and care for this lovelier flower he has created, this human soul? Have faith, Jesus says, and be as lovely as the lily of the field.

Meditation: What is beautiful, what is lasting, what is God-centered, in my life, and how shall I increase that part? How shall I learn better to worship God in the beauty of holiness.

Prayer:
>Christ of the morning,
>Christ of the dawning,
>Open my eyes to thy radiant day;
>Alone I cannot see,
>Vision derives from thee,
>Oh, give me open eyes today.
>Amen.

Week Forty
(MATTHEW 6:31–32)

Therefore take no thought, saying, What shall we eat? or, What shall we drink? or, Wherewithal shall we be clothed? (For after all these things do the Gentiles seek:) for your heavenly Father knoweth that ye have need of all these things.

To be free is mankind's noblest aim. Yet through all the centuries man has been in bondage.

In Greece, Plato envisaged an ideal republic under which men could emerge from the cave of lies and live in the sunshine of truth. In India, Gautama the Buddha taught the way to enlightenment, to freedom from the wheel of life. Modern prophets of science have predicted that knowledge and technology will free all mankind from the age-old enemies of poverty and ignorance, letting us attain the higher life of which we are capable. As knowledge expands and education spreads, as our vision of the universe enlarges, the optimists foresee that men will take advantage of new wealth and new leisure to become wiser, more humane, and more just.

Yet for all the predictions, hopes, and expectations, man remains in bondage.

Jesus himself said, "Ye shall know the truth, and the truth shall make you free." But we have not found the truth. Or if we have found it, we have chosen to ignore it.

The Buddhist scriptures tell of a man who fell gravely ill. His friends, who were wealthy, left a precious gem hidden in the sick man's clothing so that when he was healed he would have the means to live. The ill man recovered, but did not find the jewel and lived in misery and poverty for years. Finally he was reunited with his friends, who showed him the gem that had lain hidden within his clothing for all of those sad years. The Truth, the scriptures say, is like that jewel, hidden in each of us but not found.

Jesus told his listeners on the Mount that they were devoting their souls to seeking after food, drink, and clothing. The Gentiles, the non-Jews, the people not of the Book—at least they acknowledged their preoccupation. But seekers after truth, as the Jews were supposed to be, attempted to hide from God and from themselves that their treasure was really not in heaven, it was on earth. They were not ready to acknowledge that God knew their needs and would care for them. They had only to set their spirits free in the search for him.

If we look ourselves in the face, we shall admit that what we want is ease, comfort, security for ourselves and our loved ones. In his book *Power*, Bertrand Russell wrote, "The ultimate limit to the power of creeds is set by boredom, weariness, and the love of ease." He was speaking of ideologies in the political arena, primarily, but alas, what he says is valid as well for the eternal truths that would set men free.

I am glad to accept the church as a refuge from the cares of the world. I am happy enough to have Christianity as a bulwark against my doubts about the purpose of life. I accept with pleasure the beauties of the stained glass, the hymns and anthems, the altar, the flowers, the liturgy, and all of those soothing things in the church. I welcome religion as a rich added dimension to my life. But that is not the truth Jesus promised would set me free.

Liberating truth requires that I take no thought for what I shall eat or drink or be clothed with. It requires that I turn over my wants to the heavenly Father—meaning not that he shall enrich me, but rather that I shall be satisfied with whatever version of poverty he chooses to send. The truth that will set me free requires me to turn my back on this world. It is as simple as that, and as hard. In fact, it is the hardest thing in the world.

For Jesus, the truth led to Calvary. For me, God only knows where it may lead. I may never know, for I may never summon up the courage to have faith in his will. Am I courageous enough to be set free?

If I ever find that courage, I do not doubt that the promise of Jesus will be fulfilled. The truth will set me free, if my faith deserves it. I am capable of breaking these human bonds and entering the holy ground of God's will. The doorway is open. Shall I ever walk through?

Meditation: "After all these things do the Gentiles seek." What am I seeking in my life?

Prayer: O God of peace, who as taught us that in returning and rest we shall be saved, in quietness and in confidence we shall be strong: By the might of your Spirit lift us to your presence, where we may be still and know that you are God. Amen.

Week Forty-One
(MATTHEW 6:33)

But seek ye first the kingdom of God, and his righteousness; and all these things shall be added unto you.

A spiritual pilgrim who had been blessed of God to hear the Sermon on the Mount, let us imagine, seeks out Jesus and meets him face-to-face.

"Rabbi, you have said not to think about my food, drink, and clothing, but to put my heart into the search for God's kingdom. But how shall I withdraw from this world?"

"The kingdom of God is within you."

"But Master, God has put us onto this earth in human society, with tasks and duties to perform. How should I leave that world where God has placed me, and retreat into this kingdom of God that is within me?"

"Ye cannot serve both God and mammon."

"But my wife and my children, my parents? I cannot desert them."

"Seek ye first the kingdom of God and his righteousness."

"But Rabbi, I am still of flesh, I still have requirements. How shall they be satisfied?"

"All these things shall be added unto you, O you of little faith."

And the pilgrim, one suspects, went away sorrowing, for to have faith is very difficult.

Of all the figures of history and of imagination, if I were given the heaven-sent opportunity to meet and talk to just one figure from the past, it would be Jesus. Well, that is not surprising, and perhaps most people would say the same. But I wonder, in asking to meet Jesus, to look into his compassionate eyes as did the pilgrim I have just described—I wonder what we would be seeking?

I know that when I am at a divine service, I look to the clergy for inspiration, fatherly guidance, for something to look up to. Kneeling at the altar rail, I like to feel that the clergy represent not sinful man but the cleansed and holy part of our nature. Somehow I expect that when they administer the sacrament, or lay on hands, or render a blessing, that something cleaner and purer will come into my soul from theirs. Their sacred representation speaks to my profane nature and makes me more sacred.

If I were to see Jesus, I would be in that same spirit of the anticipation of blessing. I would kneel before him in praise and wonder, expecting from those nail-pierced hands a miracle of cleansing as they touched my sinful head. I would expect that his cleanliness would make me clean.

And that is a lovely image.

But if I were blessed with the possibility of meeting Jesus—and after all, is that not what the divine service is for, to draw us close to the Master?—I would still be faced with the necessity, afterward, of living with myself in the profane world outside the temple. Even with the blessing of Jesus making a halo around my head where he had touched it— and I like to think that this is how we emerge from the communion service—I would still have to emerge into the world again.

And what then? If I have sought the kingdom of God and his righteousness, with utter sincerity, with cordial dedication, with as much faith as I am capable of—how do I take the kingdom back with me into the world? Even if I try to pray without ceasing, how shall I carry the touch of Jesus back into the traffic, the transactions, and the turmoil of my every day? How shall I link the kingdom with quotidian reality?

Jesus said, "All these things shall be added unto you." This is the mystery of faith carried over into daily life. He did not say that if I renounce the world, then God in recompense will make me high up in the world. The giving up means renouncing expectation. It means that I shall not desire riches, power, or the things of this world; and if those things come my way, I shall pass them by, or turn them over to others, or shall pay no attention to them. It is dying to this world that is crucial, and I cannot do that by half. So the secret of Jesus is: Give up the world, and you shall be free of the world.

He leaves that promise with us like the blessing of his hands on our heads, the richest gift of God.

In Washington, D.C., if you walk along the Potomac River on the Virginia shore, you can see, almost simultaneously, the tributes to six Presidents: the Washington monument, the Lincoln and Jefferson memorials, Theodore Roosevelt Island, and the Johnson grove. And up the hill behind you is another monument, in a sense, to another great American: the Lee mansion.

Standing there, I love to lift my eyes to the north, beyond Arlington and Georgetown, and see, on the highest piece of land in the District of Columbia, the magnificent National Cathedral. To me, the cathedral looms over that city of power as a reminder that beyond power, beyond politics, beyond great success in a worldly race, lies the eternal. Even amid the churning politics of Washington, the listening ear can hear the lasting words of Jesus: "Seek ye first the kingdom of God."

Meditation: How shall I master my desires, and rise above them, and yet work in this world as God would have me work? That is the challenge of the ages.

Prayer: Father, I ask that thy hands be placed upon my head in blessing, and the touch of those hands will remind me of your promise that if I can sacrifice self, I may enter into the kingdom. Help me on the way. Amen.

Week Forty-Two
(MATTHEW 6:34)

Take therefore no thought for the morrow: for the morrow shall take thought for the things of itself. Sufficient unto the day is the evil thereof.

Two hundred years ago, in 1785, a Scot was plowing a field on a November day and turned up with his plow a field-mouse and her nest. In "To a Mouse," Robert Burns wrote his unforgettable lines:

> . . . The best-laid schemes o' mice an' men
>   Gang aft agley,
> An' leave us nought but grief an' pain
>   For promis'd joy!
>
> Still thou art blest compar'd wi' me!
> The present only toucheth thee:
> But och! I backward cast my ee'
> On prospects drear!
> An' forward tho' I canna see,
>   I guess an' fear!

Although it is the stuff of every nation's poetry and song, and although every person feels in his soul the dread of looking forward, perhaps no one ever put it more memorably than Burns. But it is the secret of the human condition, this ability to see forward to our own end as a living inhabitant of this earth, and it is what makes us what we are.

Even the most devout believer in any age has stood in the fear of death. And the sensitive soul finds himself envying the birds, trees, and animals because, to the best of our knowledge, they cannot share this foreknowledge of their end. That is the fruit of the tree of the knowledge of good and evil. That is what makes us sentient, and prescient, and human. We see what is coming.

From this knowledge comes all faith, all philosophy, and every purposeful act of men and women who shape their lives in preparation for the end of it. Not long ago I visited the Episcopal Bishop of South Carolina in his offices, and found that one entire wall was glass, and gave a view of the church cemetery; the tombstones were those of his close companions. He reminded me that John Donne had kept his own coffin in readiness, as a reminder of the end, and said that he found the companionship of the tombstones comforting and useful spiritually. That reminded me of an epitaph I read on a tombstone in a little Anglican churchyard in an English village years ago, of a man who had died full of years: "Nicholas Vase. We all do fade as a leaf." That is the calm we all aspire to, as we contemplate the future and our own demise: to know that the coffin is waiting, and that we shall fall from the tree of life like a leaf which has served its purpose, whose time for falling has come.

That is what we aspire to. Philosophers and saints have no doubt attained that level of wisdom, resignation, and expectation—Spinoza seeing life "under the aspect of eternity," Marcus Aurelius seeing death as a natural part of life and nothing to dread, the Christian martyrs accepting death gladly for and in their faith. But most men and women, even in ages of far greater faith than ours, have found it hard scrambling to reach even a small hilltop of serenity. Most of us live in the valley of the shadow of death, or wallow in the slough of despond. Like the great Scots poet, we look ahead in fear, and envy the blind.

From this fear, men have recoiled through the centuries in a variety of ways. The hedonists have said that if life is short and death is sure, enjoy life to the hilt while we may: "*Gaudeamus igitur, juvunes dum sumus.*" Or like old Omar Khayyam, the purveyor of the bittersweet wine:

> Ah, make the most of what we yet may spend,
> Before we too into the Dust descend.

Some stay busy and look away from the future. Others pretend they are immune. All manner of ways, men cope, or fail to cope.

And above and beyond all of this, even in our age of little faith, towering over the wrecks of time, Jesus stands on the mountain in Galilee and tells us that the evil of each day is enough for that day. Tomorrow will care for itself. That dread of the morrow is a waste of the fruit of life; the future is in God's hands.

Jesus says this, and most of the time we fail to listen. We are so busy putting away thoughts of our mortal future that we fail to heed the words of the Master of Death. So busy with pastimes that we do not listen to the words of him who transcends time and mortality.

But if we stop and listen, the voice of Christ is to be heard, quiet but sure, cutting through the debris of the centuries, the ruins of our lives, saying that we should not look ahead in fear, but should put our fears on the altar of God, where they will be sanctified and will no longer hurt us. Jesus speaks, and time, death, and eternity listen. Can I listen too?

Meditation: Can I look down the avenue of my life and see a cross, and then stand back, and hear the words of the Savior, and find my tears for myself dried in the comfort of his embrace?

Prayer: In an age of unbelief, Lord, help my unbelief. Give me grace to see beyond my own mortality. Give me strength to put my tomorrows into the hands of a loving God. Amen.

Week Forty-Three
(MATTHEW 7:1–5)

> *Judge not, that ye be not judged. For with what judgment ye judge, ye shall be judged: and with what measure ye mete, it shall be measured to you again. And why beholdest thou the mote that is in thy brother's eye, but considerest not the beam that is in thine own eye? Or how wilt thou say to thy brother, Let me pull out the mote out of thine eye; and behold, a beam is in thine own eye? Thou hypocrite, first cast out the beam out of thine own eye; and then shalt thou see clearly to cast out the mote out of thy brother's eye.*

And Jesus, sorrowing, looked at the men and women scattered before him on the Mount, and beyond them to all of mankind: those who had been, those who were, and who were to be. He saw that we are all prisoners, each chained in the dungeon of his own brain by the bonds of self. Unable to rise above that prison cell, we see the world only through selfish eyes, detecting all the sins and shortcomings of others, overlooking those within ourselves. And because we lack compassion, fellow-feeling, we are condemned to our chains. Yet as dissemblers and hypocrites, from our very bondage we continue to proclaim our own virtues.

But Jesus, ever compassionate, felt within our hypocritical hearts the desire to be better men and women. He told us we might be free. The way to strike off our chains and to emerge free into the sunlight, Jesus said, is to look at ourselves as we look at others. If we can perceive our own faults, and ask forgiveness for them, in that act we will gain mercy, and help our brothers and sisters to freedom as well.

Yet how hard it is for us to abjure the role of righteous judge! Our English word "hypocrite" comes directly from the Greek word *hypokrites*, or "actor"; and we all do love to be holier than those around us. As parents, we stand in stern judgment of our small children. As brothers and sisters and children, we all too often are ready to criticize siblings and parents. As members of society, we pronounce bitter anathema upon those who are more privileged than we, and upon those who are less privileged; in both cases we argue that they, unlike us, do not "deserve" what they have. As members of a nation, we peer across international borders and proclaim others to be aggressive, unfair, evil, or militaristic, while pretending that our own nation is spotless.

But Jesus Christ went up on a mountain in Galilee and said, majestically, "Judge not, that ye be not judged."

Jesus said we have the power within us to strike off our chains and stand free of bondage to self, free of the pretension to holiness, free of the sin of condemning a fellow human being.

In that goodly Christmas sermon, *A Christmas Carol*, Scrooge made an awful remark about decreasing the surplus population, and the Ghost said how pitiful it was for the insect on the leaf to pronounce judgment on his fellow insect in the dust.

Do you suppose that Jesus actually expects me to give up the comfort of my feeling of moral superiority? The feeling that I deserve to live in a rich country, with all the comforts of twenty-first-century technology, while millions on the same planet live without possessions, in the daily knowledge of hunger? The feeling that by voting, reading the daily paper, and belonging to a civic club or neighborhood association I have a right to membership in the League of the Satisfied? The feeling that while my brother seems to have a speck of dust obstructing his vision, and should get it out of his eye, that large piece of wood blocking my sight is nothing to be concerned about?

But Jesus said, "Quit acting. Quit pretending. Stand away from the judgment seat. The head bowed in shame is the head that shall be erect in freedom."

Meditation: If I look at myself through the eyes of God, first seeing myself in my own city, and then from a higher distance seeing myself on my own continent, and then from still higher seeing myself as the tiniest speck on a small cloud-encircled blue planet—if I see myself in that perspective, shall I not see more truly my own small place in God's universe?

Prayer: The Almighty and merciful Lord grant all of us absolution and remission of our sins, true repentance, amendment of life, and the grace and consolation of his Holy Spirit. Amen.

Week Forty-Four
(MATTHEW 7:6)

Give not that which is holy unto the dogs, neither cast ye your pearls before swine, lest they trample them under their feet, and turn again and rend you.

Jesus reminds us of the beauty and sanctity of life.

I do not know whether it was harder for the listeners to the Sermon on the Mount, living under alien rule in cruel times, to remain aware of the holiness of life, or harder for us today. Perhaps it is only a blest minority who can keep themselves attuned to the beauty of holiness. Surely it is a very hard thing to do in any day.

Personally, I like to think of education as a pearl. In ancient times, the educated man was the one who went on beyond the physical to the metaphysical, the one who acquired a philosophy in its true meaning, the love of wisdom. How many mature men and women today, who are exposed to the great ideas of mankind, have left their ideas in the classroom and live in a world barren of metaphysics or philosophy? Is this not casting the pearl of education on the ground, among the pigs?

And if we think of ethics and morality, we must acknowledge that in this terrible twentieth century—armed with more brutal weapons, equipped by technology for greater control over masses of men, inspired by inhumane ideologies—we have fallen away from the ideals of earlier ages and have hurt more men, women, and children than ever before. To think of the millions of suffering people during this century is to shudder with repulsion—people on every continent, of nearly every race and color. I think of the whites' mistreatment of the blacks in my own native South; the German treatment of the Jews under Hitler; the communist Russian regime's treatment of its own people; the plight of the Chinese under the Japanese; the fate of Cambodians, Armenians, Crimean Tatars, Kurds, Ugandans, and—and the list is endless. We have forgotten the sanctity of life. Is not this casting that which is holy unto the dogs?

If we think of sharing the God-given wealth of our small, blue planet, then we must acknowledge the awful inequalities that give some people the ultimate in luxury, while most of the rest suffer in poverty and despair. The danger of despoiling our common homeland, the earth, seems to grow with the burgeoning population. Our world, which should be a temple to God, has been abused. Is not this casting a pearl of great price before swine?

If we think of the ugliness of twentieth-century life that we are compelled to live with—the pornography, the spoiling of the countryside and the cityscape, the corruption of the popular arts like television and cinema, the paving over of the green places of escape—then we must acknowledge that we have made it much harder to find refuge in calm and tranquility, harder to find God, harder to lead the life of the spirit. Is this not handing a holy thing to dogs?

The voice of Jesus sounds down the mountainside and along the pavement of our modern cities, saying that the pearl of holiness is still beyond price. He says that there is in mankind still the seed of the love of wisdom, a longing for justice, a cherishing of beauty. He says that men still want to worship God in the beauty of holiness. He says that we still wish to enter into the calm of the temple and to leave behind the profane world.

If we do not listen to those better urgings within us, we shall pay a terrible price. Our Lord said not only that it was a great waste, a profanation, to give what was holy to the dogs, to cast pearls before swine. He also said that if we did that, the pigs would conquer; they would turn on us, and trample our beautiful pearls, and then fall upon us.

Injustice, poverty, ugliness—these are not merely unfortunate happenings on the human road. They are the result of our refusal to recognize the sanctity of life. We cannot serve both God and mammon. If we choose mammon, mammon will be king, and mammon will turn and rend us. Is this not the choice our century has made?

Meditation: What is holy in my life? What do I do to keep it holy?

Prayer: Lord, keep my eyes fixed on the beauty of holiness, and let me try to reflect that beauty in my life. Amen.

Week Forty-Five
(MATTHEW 7:7-8)

Ask, and it shall be given you; seek, and ye shall find; knock, and it shall be opened unto you: For every one that asketh receiveth; and he that seeketh findeth; and to him that knocketh it shall be opened.

John Bunyan begins his marvelous tale, *The Pilgrim's Progress*, "As I walked through the wilderness of this world . . ." The pilgrim fell asleep; he saw a man in rags with a burden on his back, who read, wept, and trembled, and finally broke out in a lamentable cry, "What shall I do?"

We are all of us walking through the wilderness of the world. We are all bearing our burdens, we are all weighted down and mired, we are all weeping and trembling, we are all crying out, "What shall I do?"

And from the mountain above the Sea of Galilee the Master sees our woes, and hears our cries, and utters with the calm of timelessness that astounding assurance, "Ask, and it shall be given you; seek, and ye shall find; knock, and it shall be opened unto you."

Amazingly, Jesus says that receiving is not a matter of concern, finding is not a problem: Asking is the problem. In the wilderness of this world, we have his assurance that if we ask, what we ask will be given. The terrible question is *what* to ask.

We each wander our own way through the wilderness, and each of us must decide for what we will ask. The awful part is that in asking, we determine the answer. We are doomed or destined to find what we seek.

What if I ask, "What shall I do to be rich?" God help me, if I mean it—if I truly want to be rich more than anything else in the world—then, Jesus says, I shall be given riches. But the treasure comes not without a great price; in finding riches, I may lose my soul. "What shall if profit a man, if he gain the whole world, and lose his own soul?"

"What shall I do to survive?" is the driving question of many. Their part of the wilderness of this world may be so severe, so oppressive, whether physically or psychologically, that they are in danger of going under, and they may only have strength to pray for survival. Let no one judge the prayer.

"What shall I do to be free?" Walking to my office one morning, along the river front, I saw two swifts darting and careening in the air. Perhaps they were only catching their breakfast, but a graceful thing they made of getting their daily food. As birds have always done to earthbound men, the swifts spoke to me of freedom. They drew my eye out over the river, where a boat was cruising downstream toward the open sea.

As I walked, I remembered going from two years in Prague—where the citizens were not only landlocked but could get no official permission to travel abroad—to my first day in Stockholm, where on a sparkling May day the Swedes were darting and careening their boats over the water like swifts in the air. It suddenly came to me that these Swedes needed no exit visas, no permission to leave; they could sail their boats, if they wanted to, to Finland or Denmark or on to England and beyond. I felt in my bones how beautiful a thing freedom is.

In this wilderness, uncounted multitudes are yearning for freedom from all kinds of bondage, whether political, economic, or personal. Jesus said if freedom is the crux of what they want, they can ask, and will receive it.

"What shall I do to be saved?" To be freed from bondage to sin and to this world and to live in the world beyond time—is not this the highest plea that we can make? But as Jesus made clear to a certain ruler who asked this question of him, it is the price of making the request that is high. If we truly want to be saved; if the miracle of rising to a higher, freer plane of existence is what we want more than anything else in life; if we are willing to put all else aside and ask for salvation: then Jesus says, simply, calmly, "It shall be given you." That is the matchless promise lying at the heart of the Sermon.

"What shall I do to serve?" Perhaps this is an even higher way to ask God for the best gift he can give. For after we have wrestled with the passions of our own sins and salvation, we must realize, if we are to follow Jesus, that burying self and asking God how to serve is the best question of all. The answer will be different for each person. Some will be told to minister to loved ones; some will be told to do pious things in private; some will be sent out into the world to give of self to others. "Seek, and ye shall find."

Meditation: What am I seeking in my life? What great distillation am I prepared to undergo in order to stand before God with my own ultimate, essential request on my lips? What shall I ask God for, bearing in mind always Christ's wonderful and terrible promise that God would give me exactly what I asked him for? What shall I do?

Prayer: Father, give me grace to ask the right gift for my life. Amen.

Week Forty-Six
(MATTHEW 7:9–11)

Or what man is there of you, whom if his son ask bread, will he give him a stone? Or if he ask a fish, will he give him a serpent? If ye then, being evil, know how to give good gifts unto your children, how much more shall your Father which is in heaven give good things to them that ask him?

To feel that we are all children of a loving God: This is the richest gift we could ask. It does not come to most of us. To those who receive it, the feeling waxes and wanes, is strong and then disappears. But the feeling is more precious than gold and rubies. It is the legacy of Christ.

The disinterested love for another human being is our highest mortal manifestation of divine love. By unselfishly loving those with whom we share the planet, we prove ourselves, to a certain degree, sons and daughters of God. Jesus chooses, probably because his congregation on the Mount was predominantly male, to use the example of fathers and sons. The example of mother love or love of daughters would be equally telling. Jesus is saying that as parents, we come as close as we shall come on earth to acting like God, that is, demonstrating pure love.

Being blessed with four dearly loved children, my wife and I know the truth of Jesus' example. When we talk about the world and its cares, we will often speak of our children. The reference may not be carefree, for everyone has concerns and problems, and as parents we naturally speak of those from time to time, with loving concern. But most of the time, mention of the children is simply an act of homage, a verbal caress, a sharing of the reassurance that there are four lovely human beings who mean more to us than our own lives. This mention invariably lifts our spirits as when weary travelers approach an inn or when a long winter breaks out into sudden spring. It is not feigned, not something you advertise: It is simply parental love, warming the heart. And the older we get, the brighter burns this flame of parental love, while other flames—ambitions, worldly interests—die down. It is the love every parent knows, and it comes without bidding from the very wellspring of the soul. I know of no sweeter human experience.

Yet I, who like to consider myself a most loving father, have shown impatience, have struck my children when they were younger, have not given the time to fatherhood that I should have. This is the human side of my nature, what Jesus called my evil side, dimming the flame of the divine, loving side.

God is pure love, Jesus said—and showed by his own example. We can rely on our heavenly Father to bestow only love upon his children. Therefore, all we need do is ask, and he will give us all good things. Could there be a more comfortable, a more glorious promise?

Who can recount all the good things God bestows? He gives the marvel of life itself. On our little, blue planet, we do not know how many other places in the universe may be blessed with life. There may be uncounted millions of life-bearing planets, or there may be very few; we do not know. When we contemplate the almost infinite majesty of God's universe, the incomprehensible distances, the ungraspable extremes of heat and cold, dark and light, and then we turn our eyes from that to the terribly finite reaches of our own little world, we shudder with awe at being given the sentience to know these unreachable reaches of existence. To be aware of ourselves in the midst of this unbounded universe—what a great gift!

God gives the miracle of human life and human relations. Jesus spoke of parents and children, that lovely bond. At times he also spoke of the great mystery of the love of husband and wife, perhaps the most splendid and the richest of all human covenants. Then there are the beautiful bonds of friendship. And the larger frameworks that bind neighborhoods, tribes, and nations together. All of the great literature of human history has only scratched the surface of the complexity of human relationships: What an unfathomable gift!

Oh, but a listing of the good things God has given us could go on and on. The joy of beauty. The vigorous pleasure of physical exercise. The satisfactions of good food and drink. The comfort of a home. The happiness of doing some challenging job well, of using our talents in the service of a high cause. The comfort of the spiritual life. The list is endless, bounded not by God's love but by our ability to perceive it and to appreciate it. The only proper response to life is to bow in wonder and thanksgiving before the Giver of all these good things.

Meditation: May I spend a profitable hour, day, or week counting over the good gifts of God.

Prayer: In and beyond all your marvelous gifts, O Father, give us the constant gift of unfeigned thanksgiving. Amen.

Week Forty-Seven
(MATTHEW 7:12)

Therefore all things whatsoever ye would that men should do to you, do ye even so to them: for this is the law and the prophets.

The Golden Rule has been revealed to mankind more than once, by Jesus and by great prophets and teachers of the ages. But men prefer not to hear.

It is a marvelously simple saying of our Lord's that we should do to others as we would have them do to us. Yet it is the hardest thing in the world: It is the secret of the universe.

If the progression of life is toward self-awareness, then the highest life is that which can be as respectful of other-life as it is of self-life. If the lion had mercy on the lamb, this would be an impossible miracle of nature, and it would soon mean a starving lion. Yet man, the hungry lion among spiritual beasts, is told, by this Preacher on the Mount, to show the same mercy to the lamb that he would have the lion show to him. Jesus asks us to break through the iron bars that cage us in our own bodies, and to place our spirits in the bodies of others. By feeling their pain, as if it were our own, we shall learn to treat them with love, even as we would wish them to treat us with love.

But how hard that is!

Two nights ago, out for my evening walk, I passed a man lying on the sidewalk just around the corner from a church. He stirred as I passed, and seemed asleep and not ill. After looking at him, I walked on in the dark, thinking about what to do. A block farther on I passed a police car. So I assuaged my conscience by telling the patrolmen about the man on the sidewalk.

Our city is not so large that people on sidewalks are a commonplace, as they are in the larger metropolises where I have lived, New York or Washington or Paris. But they are not unknown, either, and my assumption was that the man was an alcoholic, a derelict. So I told my conscience that I did the proper thing in informing the police, in case he was ill.

But as I walked on, I thought of Jesus' parable of the Good Samaritan, and I thought how terribly hard it would have been for me to lift up that man, whoever or whatever he was, and to take him to my house, which was only a half-block away. I need not tell you that I conjured up dozens of reasons why in the twentieth century my behavior was understandably different from that of the Good Samaritan in Jesus' time. They failed to persuade me. I did not obey the Golden Rule, explain my failure away as I will.

I do not know about you, but I am most ingenious in finding examples to parade before my own eyes of ways in which I do good, ways in which I obey the Golden Rule, ways in which I might stake out some claim to righteousness. I am even more ingenious in closing my eyes to the myriad times that I fail to do unto others as I would have them do unto me. I have discovered how to leave those in quietness, unnoticed.

There is a series on the local television news showing retarded and handicapped children, asking families to adopt them. Cherishing the middle-class privacy and comfort of my own home, I do not consider such a thing. There are appeals at our church for members to work in the local soup kitchen, to give time for visiting local jails and prisons. I find ample excuses for being too busy for that. There are those who give their lives to help the sick and the poor, but I do not manage to give even an hour. There are many people who tithe, or who give a large proportion of their money to charity or to good causes; but I seem to find ways to spend my money without having a great deal left over for giving.

How many people do I come in contact with on my weekly rounds who are in need of comforting, friendship, or encouragement, whom I could help? How many hurts are there that I could cure, if I would do to those hurt people as I would have them do to me? What good is there I might do in this world of sorrow, if I would but do it?

The trick, of course, is to interpret Jesus' words very narrowly, and to find ways to excuse myself from the application of the Golden Rule. But Jesus' words hang heavy in our hearts, do they not? "All things whatsoever," he said. And he must have meant that in every conscious act I should try to place myself outside myself, acting for others instead of for myself. "This is the law and the prophets," he said: This is the secret heart of all my teaching.

It is so simple that it is terrifying.

Meditation: In a world of have-nots, am I guilty of being one of the haves who sit comfortably on his or her goods and will not look at those around in need? Am I guilty of finding excuses for keeping the deprived, deprived; the poor, poor; the downtrodden, downtrodden? Am I guilty of cherishing my own comfort in the delusion that I have "earned" it, forgetting that all things come from God, and that Jesus told me to put myself in my brother's shoes? How far did Jesus mean for me to take the Golden Rule in my life?

Prayer: Father, in a world of hurt and sorrow, teach me to reach out to the hurt and the sorrowful as I would have them reach out to me. Amen.

Week Forty-Eight
(MATTHEW 7:13–14)

> *Enter ye in at the strait gate: for wide is the gate, and broad is the way, that leadeth to destruction, and many there be which go in thereat: Because strait is the gate, and narrow is the way, which leadeth unto life, and few there be that find it.*

J esus is Lord of the narrow gate.

Most of us prefer the wide and well-trodden way. Jesus said it leads to destruction of life, the loss of the soul.

In Jesus' day, only a very few people were rich, in the sense that the bulk of the population is rich in the industrialized world of the twentieth century. Their silks, rich food, and luxuries are equaled or surpassed in most ways by the ordinary life afforded us today by electricity, consumer goods, and the corner supermarket. Ordinary people in America live like the rich few in Palestine of biblical times. To those few, Jesus said, "Sell what you have and give it to the poor, and seek the strait way and the narrow gate."

I can only suppose that he is saying the same thing to us today. More uncomfortable words.

What is the narrow way that Jesus told his congregation on the Mount to follow? Was it not the path to the kingdom of heaven, which lay in meekness, and poverty, and the aspiration for perfection? Was it not the way of the turned cheek, the forgiven trespass, the beloved enemy? Was it not the way of those who would be like God himself, pure love?

The counsel of perfection, which Jesus our Lord gave to us in the Sermon on the Mount, has stood before mankind like a great challenging boulder in its path. Some have derided the idea of the perfectibility of man, taking shelter in the concept of original sin and in the self-evident evil in every man's heart. Many have said that the sense of guilt arising from the aspiration to perfection is itself the source of human hurts, fears, and scars; therefore we should cease to strive for a manifestly impossible state of perfection, and should accept ourselves as we are, but without the burden of guilt. Others have pointed out how pernicious was the doctrine of perfectibility when it was applied to man in society, as if a certain kind of system of governance could set man free from ancient fetters and allow him to flourish in some guiltless utopia. Many wise critics have said that religion, with its setting aside of the sacred in life, with its insistence on a spiritual dedication to perfection, is a stage in history whose time has passed, so that man can now proceed on a new and guiltless way.

But Jesus stands at the angle of the centuries and says, "The road to destruction is wide, and many are in it; but the gate into life is narrow, and few find it."

Our wise Savior knew that no human being would attain to the perfect state of the Father in heaven; but he also knew that the hope of perfection—the striving to be what we should be—was what sustained life and made it holy. Jesus knew that the profane life could be led in ease and comfort, with pastimes, amusements, and diversions, with gratification of the flesh, with forgetfulness of the spirit. And he also knew that this was indeed the path to destruction. That destruction might take many forms: whole societies under despotic rule; men and women enslaved by addictive things; people so deluded by the appearance of things that they lose the capacity to experience substance; men and women deprived of those essentials of bearable human existence: faith, hope, and love.

The other path, Jesus said, is hard, rocky, thorny, and very narrow. We twentieth-century folk who pretend that the way Jesus pointed out is a pleasurable, easy road, are deluding ourselves. We like to assume that our way of life has solved the basic problems, so that the modern consumer society provides the good and comfortable life for nearly everyone. And we like to pretend that on this material foundation, a little temple of spirituality can be erected, one that will suffice for our other-worldly needs. The hard moral choices, whether in our society, on our small planet, or inside our own minds, are choices we like to think we can leave aside.

But Jesus says, "Narrow is the gate and narrow the way that leads to life; and few there be that find them." If we lose the agonizing desire for perfection, for holiness, for living within the kingdom of God, then we have lost the very foundation of spiritual happiness, which is hope. The way to life is excruciatingly difficult, but those who do not try to follow it are on the pleasant path to destruction.

Jesus is Lord of the narrow gate.

Meditation:
>The peace of God, it is no peace
>But strife closed in the sod.
>Yet, brothers, pray but for one thing—
>The marvelous peace of God.
>>William Alexander Percy
>>"They Cast Their Nets
>>in Galilee"

Prayer: Lord, lead me in the narrow way. Amen.

Week Forty-Nine
(MATTHEW 7:15-20)

> *Beware of false prophets, which come to you in sheep's clothing, but inwardly they are ravening wolves. Ye shall know them by their fruits. Do men gather grapes of thorns, or figs of thistles? Even so every good tree bringeth forth good fruit; but a corrupt tree bringeth forth evil fruit. A good tree cannot bring forth evil fruit, neither can a corrupt tree bring forth good fruit. Every tree that bringeth not forth good fruit is hewn down, and cast into the fire. Wherefore by their fruits ye shall know them.*

Do you share my impression that in this twentieth century after Christ, people seeking the kingdom of heaven find themselves in a great company of false prophets?

As they sat on that hillside in Palestine and heard Jesus' Sermon, his listeners must have understood what kinds of false prophets he was warning them against. Perhaps Jesus meant the imitators of John the Baptist, some of whom proclaimed simple ways to salvation. Perhaps he meant the ever-present temptation of false gods, of religions coming from outside Israel to supplant the ancient worship of Jehovah. Perhaps he meant the political prophets, those who proclaimed Caesar as god, or those who pretended that an anti-Caesar could create the kingdom of heaven on earth.

Jesus warned against simple ways to salvation, and against false gods, and against political prophets. His listeners must have understood.

I wonder if we understand today. The company of false prophets is so vast, it seems, that we have great trouble closing our ears to them and listening to the still small voice of the true prophet. We seem to be persuaded in these latter days that we have learned how to produce grapes on thorn-trees and figs on bushes of thistles.

Who are false prophets today? From the secular community comes a host of commercial messages portraying life as a series of satisfiable hungers and happiness as gratification of our material wants. From the religious community comes a host of television evangelists, promising release from sorrow in a word, heaven without pain or trouble, and instant spiritual gratification. Some of those same messengers provide simplistic solutions to enormously complex political problems, as if conflicts of interest could be made to disappear by slogans and shibboleths.

All around us, people are saying that the pursuit of self-interest will produce a prosperous and just society, that attainment of inward contentment is the goal of the spiritual life, that the acceptance of inequality and injustice is the price of domestic tranquility, that youth and glamor are the chief components of happiness, that guilt may be banished from modern lives, that to succeed is the highest goal while to lose is almost blasphemous. And so on. These are compelling voices, at times, are they not? Is it not exceedingly difficult to turn away, and to seek the true and the hard path?

I do not say, and it would not be in the spirit of the Master to say, that all those seductive voices are those of wolves dressed like sheep. Many of them are well-meaning—even truth-seeking—men and women who would be good prophets. But in the uncomfortable words of Jesus, are not their messages false prophecies? Can the self-contented, the complacent, the hypocritical truly offer us good fruit? Is it not true that their apparent grapes and figs grow in accessible places, alongside broad thoroughfares, but when they are plucked, the taste is bitter and unsatisfying?

Jesus was hard on hypocrites. There must have been a great number of them in Galilee and Judea in his day. There are a great number of them in any day. And the trying part is that anyone who decries the hypocrites is very likely to turn out to be hypocritical himself. Jesus advised us only to cast stones when we were without sin, so we are well-advised to pocket our stones, all of us. Therefore we risk sinning even by pointing our fingers at those we consider sinners. Better to let our words be "yea" and "nay" and leave the evil to be sufficient unto itself.

Our bounden duty, nevertheless, is to seek the truth and, as Jesus told us, to beware of false prophets. The crusader against evil is all too likely to fall into the sin of self-righteousness. Jesus would have us to be keenly aware of the evil within us, and therefore to avoid being deluded by the evil in others. And he promises, at last, that if we follow the narrow path, the true fruit of the tree of life will yet be ours.

Meditation: Of what false prophecies and of which false prophets am I the prisoner?

Prayer: Father, lead me beside still waters, make me to lie down in green pastures, make whole my soul, and let me dwell in thy house forever. Amen.

Week Fifty
(MATTHEW 7:21-23)

> *Not every one that saith unto me, Lord, Lord, shall enter into the kingdom of heaven; but he that doeth the will of my Father which is in heaven. Many will say to me in that day, Lord, Lord, have we not prophesied in thy name? and in thy name have cast out devils? and in thy name done many wonderful works? And then will I profess unto them, I never knew you: depart from me, ye that work iniquity.*

The Sermon on the Mount becomes more painful as we approach its end. Like climbing a high mountain, we find the last yards the hardest as we encounter cruel stones, thin air, and dark winds. But the true pilgrim persists, for he is bound for the blessed summit, whence one may see the kingdom of God.

On the pathway that is the Sermon, the pilgrim who is trying to heed the words of the Master meets challenges to all his assumptions, as if Jesus were saying, "No, it is not so easy as that."

The pilgrim says, "Lord, if I do what I do in your name, surely that makes it good and right." But Jesus says that calling upon the name of the Lord, doing things in his name, is not enough. We must do the will of the Father in heaven.

The pilgrim says, "Lord, I have tried to do as you did: I tried to heal the sick, and do good deeds in your name." But Jesus says that the deeds we do in God's name, the deeds we believe to be the work of God, may all be wrongly directed, selfish, or irrelevant to finding the kingdom. Jesus says that discerning and then doing the will of the Father is excruciatingly difficult, not easy at all. Uncomfortable words indeed!

The pilgrim says, "Lord, I have done my best, and in your name." But Jesus says that while we may call upon his name, he may not even know us, and we may have accomplished only sin and evil. Then he voices those heart-stopping words: "Depart from me."

If God is love, and if Jesus is the heart of all compassion, can it really be true that he would say to the pilgrim who has tried to do good in his name, "Depart from me"? This is a terrible knot of incomprehension as we seek through the Sermon to touch the heart of our Lord. No one should pretend the knot is easy to untie.

I believe that Jesus is saying to all who truly desire to be pilgrims, who truly seek God's will as the pathway to his kingdom, "The narrow way is very hard to find and to traverse." He is telling us that for the mass of men—those who ignore the spiritual world, ease the conscience by half-services and half-truths, close the ears to the cries of mankind and the eyes to a Christian's duty—for them there is not such difficulty, for they are in the broad and easy way. For the few who try to penetrate life, to live more deeply than surface lives, to reach the realm of the supernatural and the sacred—for them, Jesus says, the way is agonizing, and most pilgrims fail or go astray. Yet the challenge stands: If you wish to save your soul, if you wish to find eternal life, if you wish to inherit the kingdom of heaven, then you must attempt the straight gate and the narrow path.

But then every one of us who dons the pilgrim's garb and attempts the narrow way must stand in the divine presence and ask what he or she is to do. For myself, I am sorely tempted to withdraw from this world, to seek solace in privacy and in comforting my own soul. Other pilgrims have their own temptations. Every one of us will wish to stand before the Lord and say, "Have I not done this in your name, or that in your name?" Every one of us will lay before him all the cherished evidences of the goodness of our hearts.

But Jesus replies to each of us, and his words ring loudly in each new age, "Not every one that saith unto me, 'Lord, Lord,' shall enter into the kingdom of heaven; but he that doeth the will of my Father which is in heaven."

Then we pilgrims cry out, "But Lord, I want to do the will of the heavenly Father. My heart is right. But it is hard for me to know that will. How shall I know what to do?"

Jesus replies, "If you will place your soul on the altar, and then look within it, you will find there the knowledge of the will of God. If you seek, you will find."

So at the summit of this uncomfortable pathway lies comfort, help, and a promise. The pilgrim who seeks God's will in life, truly, will find it, and will find the strength to do it.

Meditation: First I should count over to myself those many things which I profess to be in the Lord's name but which I know interiorly to be selfish. Then I should ask for guidance in discovering the will of God for my life. The strength to do the will of God, once it is found, will surely come.

Prayer: Father, forgive me my hypocrisies. Help me to know myself. Give me strength to do your will in my life. Amen.

Week Fifty-One
(MATTHEW 7:24–27)

Therefore whosoever heareth these sayings of mine, and doeth them, I will liken him unto a wise man, which built his house upon a rock: And the rain descended, and the floods came, and the winds blew, and beat upon that house; and it fell not: for it was founded upon a rock. And everyone that heareth these sayings of mine, and doeth them not, shall be likened unto a foolish man, which built his house upon the sand: And the rain descended, and the floods came, and the winds blew, and beat upon that house; and it fell: and great was the fall of it.

So Jesus comes to the end of his Sermon, telling us, in these powerful images, that those who heed his words will live in a mighty fortress, while those who heed not will live in a little house resting upon sand.

Those of us who have walked up the Mount with Jesus, and have listened carefully to the divine words, have suffered along the way, for he has told us a great many uncomfortable things; but at the end, we are given great solace, unfathomable comfort.

Deep within our souls, if we have the courage to peer within, we find an abhorrence of change, a great yearning for certainty and for something that will last. In a universe of relativity, where someplace between exploding galaxies and unstable sub-particles the mind of man yearns for an anchor and for rest, we understand with tears the twilight emotion expressed by Henry Francis Lyte in the hymn "Abide With Me."

> Change and decay in all around I see;
> O Thou who changest not, abide with me.

Jesus says, "Believe in me, and listen to my sayings, and do my commandments, and I will give you a strong house to dwell in forever, a house that the rains cannot harm, and the floods cannot swallow, and the winds cannot dislodge, for it is founded upon the rock of ages."

Jesus says that however much the heart may fear the night, and the soul may be afraid of death, he can offer a place of refuge that is a haven from the storms of death and night.

Jesus says that, while the choice is hard, the gate is narrow, and the way is steep, those who take him at his word will enter into the company of the blessed and will inherit the security of the eternal.

Jesus says, "Let not your heart be troubled: ye believe in God, believe also in me. In my Father's house are many mansions: if it were not so, I would have told you. I go to prepare a place for you" (John 14:1–2). That mansion, founded on that mighty rock, is the reward to the faithful.

It is not a house of perfection, where all stress is removed and where care is a stranger. We have heard enough uncomfortable words from the Master in this great Sermon to know that his way is the way of the cross, the way of perplexing and continuing demands, the way of challenge. A mansion of total repose would not be a place of spiritual rest, it would be a place of decay. In the world of Jesus, the kingdom of heaven is surrounded by the world of mammon, and the tension between the two is never-ending.

But to the lost spirit wandering in the darkness of this earthly kingdom, Jesus shines a great light. He shows to that lost spirit the limitations of death; that the loving heart can rise above and encompass death; that we can, by self-forgetting love, reach that marvelous plane where one's own death becomes unimportant in the great grasp of the infinity of God's love for his creation. In the light of Jesus' matchless words in the Sermon on the Mount, we see our own life and death in a new proportion to the life of the universe. We see ourselves as an extension of the life of God himself. We see our lives as a manifestation of the great central Life that animates the universe.

And thus we find peace.

We do not find perfection, but we embrace the hope of it. We do not find an escape from death, but we find a way to embrace it and rise above it. We do not find an exit from the suffering of mankind, but we find a way to shape our lives in accordance with the needs of our fellowman.

And at the end of the day, as we come down off the mountain, we are bound to be afraid as the dark descends, as the magic subsides, and the depressing daily realities of life beset us again. We are bound to be afraid as the rains of life start up and the winds blow around us in the dark night of the soul. We are bound to long for security in a world of change and decay.

That is when Jesus says quietly, "If you have listened to me, and do what I have said, you have a mansion that I have prepared for you. It is very strong, and it will withstand all the tempests of life, and it is founded upon a rock. Be not afraid."

Meditation: As I come to the end of this beautiful Sermon, let me look closely at my own mind and heart to see if I have heard these sayings of Jesus truly, and if I am prepared to try to act on them. In the great frightening storms of life, shall I live in a house built upon sand, or shall I live in a mansion built upon a rock?

Prayer: Lord, I believe. Help my unbelief. Amen.

Week Fifty-Two
(MATTHEW 7:28–8:1)

> And it came to pass, when Jesus had ended these sayings, the people were astonished at his doctrine: For he taught them as one having authority, and not as the scribes. When he was come down from the mountain, great multitudes followed him. . . .

We have spent the day on the mountain, listening to the sayings of the Master.

I have left my shop open, let us say, and you have left your sheep untended, and we have ignored our duties and our responsibilities in the pressing world around us. We have sat on the ground, neither hungry nor thirsty, absorbed in these troubling, comforting words. Now the sun has sunk towards the crests of the Galilean hills. Light fades in the sky and on the stilled waters of the Sea of Galilee, and we make our way together back down the mountain and back into the world of men.

Have our hearts not burned within us as we looked into

those captivating eyes and listened to that voice that seemed to issue from an altar?

How many times have we exchanged glances of wonder or of fear or of pure joy as the rabbi uttered his strange teachings? How many times have we looked down at the ground, scratching idly with our finger in the sand as this teacher spoke with authority and made us feel deeply ashamed of ourselves? How many times as we listened have we said within ourselves, "Oh, if only I could seize this message and burn it into my heart and follow it every day of my life!"

But now the light is fading. The day is ending. We tried to reach Jesus, to touch his hands, but he was surrounded by those who needed him, and now he has gone off towards the lake with his disciples, and we are left to return to the world we left this morning.

You and I stop and look at each other in the twilight, and wonder if the same hope and fear is in both our hearts. We are afraid to speak, for we have been too exalted, and now we are fearful of being brought down too low. The world awaits with its shadows, duties, enticements, and traps. The experience of eternity threatens to fade with the sunlight. We wonder where we go now, what we do.

We could follow the Savior literally, take up our cross, forget the world, sacrifice self in the imitation of Christ. Some are called to do that.

We could imprison these words in our memories, be glad we heard them, but keep them as in a treasurebox, to be fondled occasionally but not to be regarded as living things. Some will do that.

Or we could go back to our world and keep the Savior's words always before us, as warning, guide, and inspiration. Some of us will do that.

If we do try to keep these words alive within us, you and I, seeking to pattern ourselves upon them as much as our strength allows, we will be prepared for challenge and discomfort. We will have the standard of perfection to measure ourselves against. We will have the challenge of choosing the kingdom of heaven over the kingdom of mammon, with all the daily sacrifices that may entail. We will have the burden that love imposes. We shall not be comfortable, but we will have the knowledge that we are trying to follow the commandments of the Sermon.

And if we persevere, Jesus has promised comfort amid discomfort, peace amid tribulation, and the assurance of truth amid a world of false appearances. Jesus has said that the meek, the forgiving, and the poor in spirit will endure much, but that the ultimate blessedness will be theirs.

Our day is ending, but we will not forget, *surely* we will not forget, the hearing of these eternal words.

The challenge of them rises up before us now like a cross reared against the sky.

And the peace they contain lies within our memories like a blessing from the hand of the Lord. Light from Light.

Meditation: What if I had been in Galilee that day? . . . What if I were there today?

Prayer: Father, thank you for the gift of these words. Help me to remember them. Amen.